BRITISH SIGN LANGUAGE

A Beginner's Guide

BRITISH SIGN LANGUAGE

A Beginner's Guide

Dorothy Miles

BBC BOOKS

This book accompanies the BBC Television series
British Sign Language, first broadcast on BBC 1 in Spring 1988

Sign language photography specially taken by Tony Timmington (cover: front/top centre and bottom; back/bottom left and right; pp. 44-106) and Luke Finn (cover; front/top left and right; Programme Notes)

Published to accompany a series of programmes prepared in consultation with the BBC Continuing Education Advisory Council

About the Authors

Dorothy Miles is a writer, lecturer and poet in both her first and second languages, English and British Sign Language. She holds a BA in English from Gallaudet College in the USA and an MA in Educational Theatre. She has published a teachers' manual for BSL, a monograph on deaf theatre and a book of poetry which she herself performs in sign language.

Paddy Ladd has worked in all sections of the deaf community in youth and social work, with the BDA and NUD, in sign language linguistics and extensively in video and television, including the BBC TV series *See Hear*.

Acknowledgments

This book would not have been possible without the help of our fellow deaf; and of those hearing people who took the time to study and learn sign languages. And it would not have been completed without the help, advice and enthusiasm of Peter Dunkley. The authors would also like to thank the BBC Continuing Education team, who made the television series; Jennie Allen and Frank Holland of BBC Books; and Sheila Millington without whose word processor we would all have been lost.

Published by BBC Books, an imprint of BBC Worldwide Publishing,
BBC Worldwide Ltd, Woodlands, 80 Wood Lane, London W12 0TT
First published 1988
Reprinted 1988 (three times), Reprinted 1989
Reprinted 1990 (twice), Reprinted 1991
Reprinted 1992 , Reprinted 1993 (twice)
Reprinted 1994, Reprinted 1995
Reprinted 1996, Reprinted 1997 (twice)
Reprinted 1998, Reprinted 1999, Reprinted 2000
Reprinted 2001, Reprinted 2002

ISBN 0 563 21134 2
ISBN 0 563 21395 7

This book is set in 10/12 Palatino Linotron 202
Typeset in England by Phoenix Photosetting, Chatham, Kent
Printed and bound in Great Britain by The Bath Press, Bath

Foreword to *British Sign Language: A Beginner's Guide* by HRH The Princess of Wales

As Patron of The British Deaf Association, I am well aware of the place of British Sign Language in the lives of deaf people. It is not only their first language, it is at the heart of their culture, just as the English language is at the heart of ours.

The series of BBC TV programmes that this guide accompanies provides an opportunity for hearing people to become acquainted with this fascinating visual language and to learn it for themselves. It is an opportunity also to remove some of the barriers that exist between deaf and hearing people and to develop a greater understanding between us all.

As a student of British Sign Language myself, I particularly welcome this imaginative series of programmes and am delighted to be associated with this *Beginner's Guide*.

CONTENTS

INTRODUCTION

Deafness and deaf people can be seen from two points of view: the medical and the sociocultural. From the medical point of view, the deaf person is disabled and requires treatment or technological aid to correct the disabling condition. This approach is suitable for those whose hearing loss comes after they have acquired a spoken language and become used to a sound-based way of life. Such people include those who lose their hearing through illness, accident, exposure to noise, the belated effects of heredity and the process of ageing.

But what happens when a child is born profoundly deaf or becomes deaf so early that there is no memory of sound? He or she will grow up accepting soundlessness as normal, and adapt by using vision in place of hearing. In families where the parents are themselves deaf, this usually means that the child's first language will be a visual one – a sign language – and hearing children born into these families likewise begin life with a sign language. Such deaf and hearing people in Britain form the core of a sociocultural group – the British Sign Language community.

Deaf children from these families have traditionally carried their native visual language into their schools, where they meet with the much larger group of deaf children who come from hearing families. These latter children, deprived of communication in the home because they cannot pick up a spoken language in the usual way, quickly learn from their schoolmates the first language they have had full access to and make it their own. British Sign Language (BSL) thus becomes a vital factor in the many shared attitudes and experiences of deaf people that bring them together in adulthood to maintain the deaf community, a community which gathers in clubs, at social and sports events, and in national organisations.

Since the BSL cultural minority lives within an English-speaking majority, its members need to learn English literacy (reading and writing) to survive. Oral skills (speech and lipreading) are useful, but in practice they are not so easy to acquire nor can they always be used effectively in real-life situations. The educational establishment, believing that the use of BSL was itself a barrier to the acquisition of a written/spoken language, has attempted to suppress it by various means which are described in this book. In fact, despite being taught in what is their second language (English), the deaf children of deaf parents who acquire BSL in infancy often achieve a good standard of English literacy and a noticeably confident social adjustment. However, because they are given no formal tuition in BSL whatsoever, their use of it outside the classroom receives no proper guidance and so fluctuates from generation to generation and from place to place. Educators then point to these inconsistencies as proof that BSL does not work, and the children become confused about what language they are using – BSL, English or a mixture of the two. Many of the children who do not have access to BSL in infancy in fact fail to acquire adequate proficiency in *either* language.

All this indicates the need for a bilingual approach to deaf education, where BSL is used to build up comprehension and self-expression, and English is then taught as a second language. At all events, BSL *is* a language, a language that has developed and been maintained in a community of profoundly deaf adults in the face of sustained efforts to eliminate it. It is the basis of the visual culture of this community, with its traditions of storytelling, humour, drama and signed translations of English hymns, poems and songs. This culture could be far richer, and could contribute greatly to the wider culture, if BSL were to be universally recognised as the resourceful, logical and fascinating language it really is, and be allowed to flourish side by side with English.

Profoundly deaf people, seen from the medical point of view, can only hope to become imperfect hearing people. But seen as a cultural group they could develop a greater sense of identity, not only in themselves and within their community, but as respected citizens of the country they live in.

Dorothy Miles, January 1988

1
THE DEVELOPMENT OF THE DEAF COMMUNITY

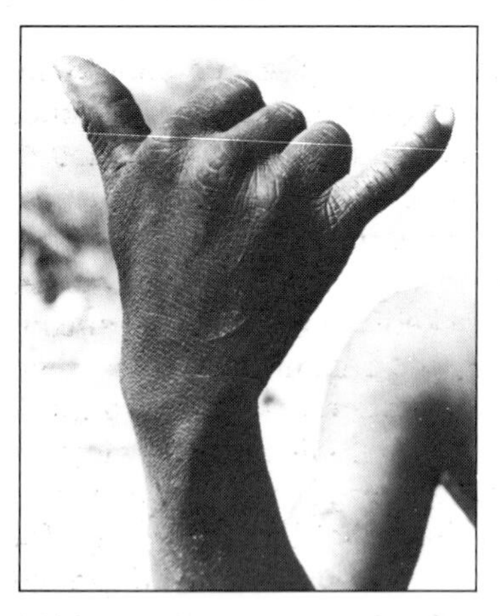

Bushman signs for 'lion' (top) and 'wildebeest' (bottom).

Introduction

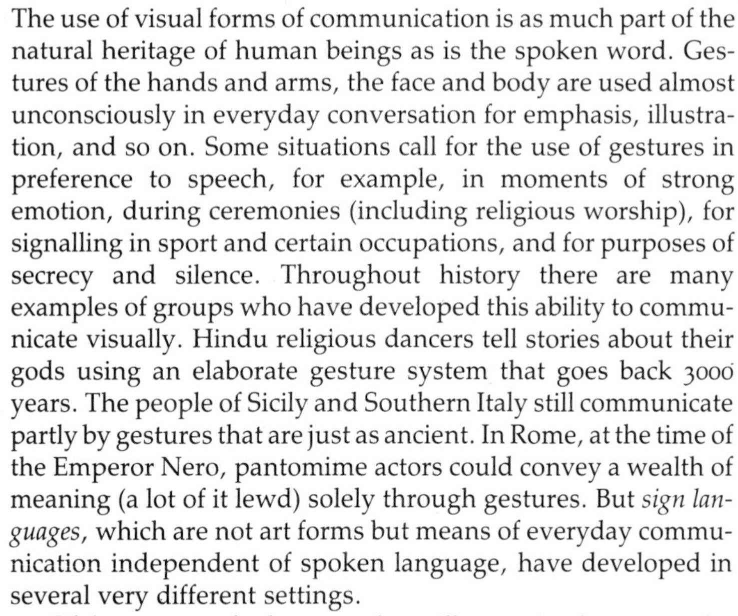

The use of visual forms of communication is as much part of the natural heritage of human beings as is the spoken word. Gestures of the hands and arms, the face and body are used almost unconsciously in everyday conversation for emphasis, illustration, and so on. Some situations call for the use of gestures in preference to speech, for example, in moments of strong emotion, during ceremonies (including religious worship), for signalling in sport and certain occupations, and for purposes of secrecy and silence. Throughout history there are many examples of groups who have developed this ability to communicate visually. Hindu religious dancers tell stories about their gods using an elaborate gesture system that goes back 3000 years. The people of Sicily and Southern Italy still communicate partly by gestures that are just as ancient. In Rome, at the time of the Emperor Nero, pantomime actors could convey a wealth of meaning (a lot of it lewd) solely through gestures. But *sign languages*, which are not art forms but means of everyday communication independent of spoken language, have developed in several very different settings.

Of the groups who have used or still use a sign language, the most notable are various aboriginal tribes, monks of the Benedictine order and deaf people – a very mixed bag! The aborigines of Australia developed their sign language for use in hunting, and at other times when speech is not permitted. The bushmen of the Kalahari Desert also used theirs for hunting, and in trade. The Plains Indians of North America (our familiar Red Indians) did more than raise their right hands and say 'How'. They developed their sign language to the point where they could tell long stories at formal gatherings. The presence of sign languages amongst these aboriginal people suggests that their use goes back to prehistoric Man.

Coming a little closer, for the past 1400 years monks belonging to religious orders first founded by St Benedict (AD 529) have been required to take a vow of partial or perpetual silence. But though words were considered unacceptable, signs were not, and certain signs were created and passed along. Many monasteries still have a thriving sign language, though it has been restricted by monastic rules and by the fact that it is not the users' main language. Deaf people are the only group for whom there is no fully satisfactory alternative to visual-gestural communication. From this natural human resource, far more natural to them than the unheard word, they have developed the most sophisticated sign languages of all. I will try here to trace that development.

Early History

Though visual communication is the natural resource of deaf people, this does not mean that a sign language springs fully developed from the hands of each deaf person. Every language is acquired through interaction with others who use it, beginning in childhood. When an individual is isolated from other people, he does not develop language skills in the normal way even if he is not deaf, as we know from reports about 'wild children', children who developed outside society and thereafter never used speech or signs.

It isn't difficult to imagine the lives led by deaf persons in the distant past. Isolated as they were, within their own families and communities as well as from each other, they each had to build communication piecemeal, out of natural gestures, mimed actions and imitated face and mouth movements. Those around them, with whom they were trying to communicate, were just as likely to show mockery or hostility as encouragement. Only in a few cases would a deaf person find non-deaf companions with enough motivation and ability to think visually, to be able to join him in developing communication beyond immediate needs. In 1779, a deaf Frenchman, Pierre Desloges, made an observation that must have been true for thousands of years previously, '. . . for those who are deprived of the company of other deaf persons . . ., or isolated somewhere in the provinces, [sign communication is] limited to physical things and bodily needs.' This language deprivation helps to explain why deaf people were for so long considered feeble-minded and legally incompetent.

There is one place, however, where the deaf person is not alone. That is within a family where several members are deaf, for such a family forms a small community of its own. The potential for creating or developing a sign language is enhanced in a family, and mutual support makes each deaf member more assured and assertive than the isolated individual. The motivation for non-deaf family members, particularly children of deaf parents, to learn sign language is also increased. The presence of deaf families even before the fourth century AD is revealed in *Talmud*, the Hebrew book which recorded the rabbis' interpretations of Jewish law. Here it was recognised that 'a deaf-mute can hold conversation by means of gestures', a statement that suggests such conversations were interpreted to the eminent rabbis by hearing family members. Deaf people were permitted to marry (and divorce) by gesture, and among the possible matches considered were those of two deaf brothers from one family to two deaf sisters from another, indicating that this happened often enough to need discussing. There must thus have been quite a number of deaf families scattered among the various Jewish communities nearly 2000 years ago. But this apparent acceptance of sign language did not mean that deaf people had full status. Speech was held to be sacred in religious ceremonies and legal dealings, and as they 'could not recite the formulae' they were not eligible to participate.

This attitude towards speech and deaf people was also prevalent in the Roman Code of Justinian in the sixth century AD, which gave legal rights only to those who could speak. This code in turn influenced many that came after it right up to the present day. By the Middle Ages, the growth of urban areas was bringing lower-class families and individuals in from country areas to find work. Thus more deaf people began to live in close proximity to each other. In the streets of the towns and cities they were able to discover each other, establish communication, gather together to form a loose community, and develop a mutual and increasingly sophisticated sign language – regardless of the fact that it was not legally accepted. Desloges, again describing what must have been a typical situation even before this, notes the effect of the deaf community on a newcomer:

> In such a theatre [Paris] our ideas develop, and when the isolated deaf man arrives he learns to polish and organise his signing, which was formerly without order and linkage. Dealing with his comrades, he quickly learns the supposedly difficult art of portraying all his thought, even the most abstract. I ought to be believed, as this is what happened to me.

Sixteenth and Seventeenth Centuries

Spain

The low status of deaf people, both socially and legally, would not have been of great concern among members of the working class, where nobody's status was very high. So concern first arose, or was made evident, among noblemen in the sixteenth century and apparently primarily among those in Spain. Generations of inbreeding had resulted in the spread of hereditary deafness among many noble families at that time, but Spanish law, like the Justinian Code, forbade deaf persons without speech to inherit titles and land. The Spanish grandees looked around for a way of protecting their assets. They may have taken inspiration from the life of Juan Fernandez de Navarrete, who was court painter to King Philip II of Spain from 1568 till his death in 1579. He was born, hearing, to a wealthy family at Logrono, but an illness left him deaf at three, and he soon stopped using speech. In later years he was known as *El Mudo* – The Mute. Fortunately, he had a natural aptitude for drawing, and was sent to be educated in art at the Hieronymite Convent of La Estrella near his home. His tutor taught him signs to add to the vocabulary he had already devised, and the two communicated in this way.

Juan Fernandez de Navarrete (El Mudo).

El Mudo completed his education by travelling and working in Italy, and is thought to have studied at the studio of Titian. When Philip II decided to build El Escorial, a monastery and administrative centre near Madrid, he chose El Mudo 'to create many paintings, glorifying the lives of Jesus and the Saints'. These El Mudo produced along with many other works elsewhere, and was considered the greatest painter of that time – 'the Spanish Titian'. When he died at the early age of 53, Spain's foremost poet Lope de Vega wrote in his honour:

Detail from 'Adoration of the Shepherds' by El Mudo. The 'signing' poses of Mary and Jesus are unique in religious painting.

Heaven stopped my tongue,
So that my speechless fashion
Might show the greater passion
That through my paintbrush sung.
Into each scene I drew,
Poured life and soul and meaning;
Thus in the silence, gleaming,
Paint spoke for me anew.

Various accounts of Juan Fernandez' life show that he used signs with everyone, even the King, and was also able to find interpreters to verify formal business dealings. We do not know if these interpreters were personal friends or came from deaf families known to El Mudo, but their presence was fully accepted by the other parties in the different transactions. They were required to swear to their interpretation of the wishes of both parties, and this interpreting made El Mudo's sign language legally acceptable. In fact, the absence of a sworn interpreter at the painter's deathbed caused legal problems over his will. El Mudo wrote down his wishes briefly and explained the details through signs, but the courts could not validate these without a formal interpretation in Spanish (though the executors went ahead and carried them out).

It was this kind of legal restriction that Spanish noblemen probably hoped to forestall when they turned to the church for help in tutoring their children, as El Mudo's parents had done. The man they chose was a Benedictine monk, Pedro Ponce de Leon, who thus became the first acknowledged teacher of the deaf. His job was to teach his pupils to speak, and later to write, sufficiently well to comply with legal requirements, and this he seems to have done with reasonable success, since he continued to get pupils for many years. As a Benedictine, Ponce de Leon would have been familiar with monastic sign language,and this must have helped him to establish communication with his pupils before he introduced them to Spanish. Unfortunately – and rather strangely – he left no record of his work, so that those who came after him in Spain and elsewhere knew only that deaf people could be taught something of a spoken and written language. This recognition was a step forward in terms of the status of deaf people, but in the long run it was to come into conflict with their determination to retain what they knew to be their natural language – sign language.

England

After Spain, the next country to become interested in the idea of teaching speech to the deaf was England. But long before such teaching was formally established, there are reports of deaf individuals who were communicating effectively by visual means. The earliest such report was in Carew's *Survey of Cornwall*, written from 1580 onwards and published in 1602. Describing the town of Saltash, he mentions

> . . . one Grisling, deaf from a long time, who besides his merry conceits of counterfeiting by signs (like the Roman pantomimi) any kind of occupation or exercise, hath a strange quality to understand what you are saying by marking the moving of your lips, especially if you speak deliberately . . .

Richard Carew.

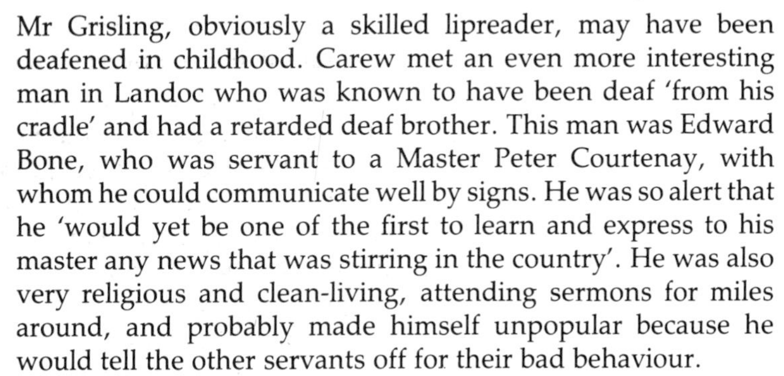

Mr Grisling, obviously a skilled lipreader, may have been deafened in childhood. Carew met an even more interesting man in Landoc who was known to have been deaf 'from his cradle' and had a retarded deaf brother. This man was Edward Bone, who was servant to a Master Peter Courtenay, with whom he could communicate well by signs. He was so alert that he 'would yet be one of the first to learn and express to his master any news that was stirring in the country'. He was also very religious and clean-living, attending sermons for miles around, and probably made himself unpopular because he would tell the other servants off for their bad behaviour.

> And to make his mind known in this and all other matters he used very effectual signs, being able therethrough to receive and perform any enjoined errand. Besides, he was assisted with so firm a memory that he would not only know any party whom he had once seen for ever afterward, but also make him known to any other by some special observation and difference.

The last phrase suggests that Bone invented name signs for the people he met in ways similar to those in use today. He probably had a name sign, too, for his deaf friend Kempe, who lived close enough for the two to form a miniature deaf community:

> [The] two, when they chanced to meet, would use such kind embracements, such strange, often, and earnest tokenings, and such hearty laughters and other passionate gestures, that their want of a tongue seemed rather an hindrance to others conceiving [understanding] them than to their conceiving each other.

The fact that Carew seemed to understand Bone's 'effectual signs' to the other servants but not his 'strange . . . tokenings' to Kempe indicates that the two deaf men had a well established sign language.

Thus from Carew's disinterested observation we know that untutored deaf people at that time could and did use at least three different forms of visual communication with those around them:

1. Mime, or mime-like signs, that could be understood by hearing people.
2. Lipreading, by which some deaf people could understand hearing people.

3 Sign language, understood by other deaf people in a community, but not by most hearing people.

Some hearing people, perhaps misled by their grasp of the first kind of communication, did believe they understood sign language. A physician called John Bulwer became interested in gestures of various kinds, including ones used by orators as well as those used by deaf people. In 1644 he published *Chirologia: or the Natural Language of the Hand*, and illustrated it with drawings of typical handshapes, some of which are still used in British Sign Language (BSL) today. But Bulwer believed that signs were a universal language, as the dedication to his second book, *Philocophus, or the Deaf and Dumb Man's Tutor* (1648), shows. This book, a treatise on lipreading, was dedicated to two deaf brothers from a wealthy family, Sir Edward and Mr William Gostwick of Wellington, Bedfordshire, in these terms:

> What though you cannot express your mindes in these verball contrivances of man's invention; yet you want not Speech, who have your whole Body for a Tongue, having a language more naturall and significant which is common to you with us, to wit gesture, the general and universal language of Humane nature . . . I am full satisfied that you want nothing to be perfectly understood . . .

Bulwer gave recognition to the effectiveness of sign language as a means of communication, but his misunderstanding about its universal nature is one that has persisted to the present day.

Samuel Pepys, the diarist, who also had a close encounter with a deaf boy, did not have Bulwer's misconception. Like Carew, he found the signs 'strange', and was most impressed by the fact that several of his companions could understand them, and one even use them. His diary entry for 9th November, 1666, describes a visit to the home of a Mrs Pierce where the guests were alarmed by the news of a fire near Whitehall (this was not long after the Great Fire of London).

> By and by comes news that the fire is slackened; so then we were a little cheered up again, and to supper and pretty merry. But above all, there comes in that Dumb boy that I knew in Oliver's time, who is mightily acquainted here and with Downing, and he made strange signs of the fire and how the king was abroad, and many things they understood but I could not – which I wondering at, and discoursing with

From John Bulwer's 'Chironomia, or the Art of Manuall Rhetorique', 1644.

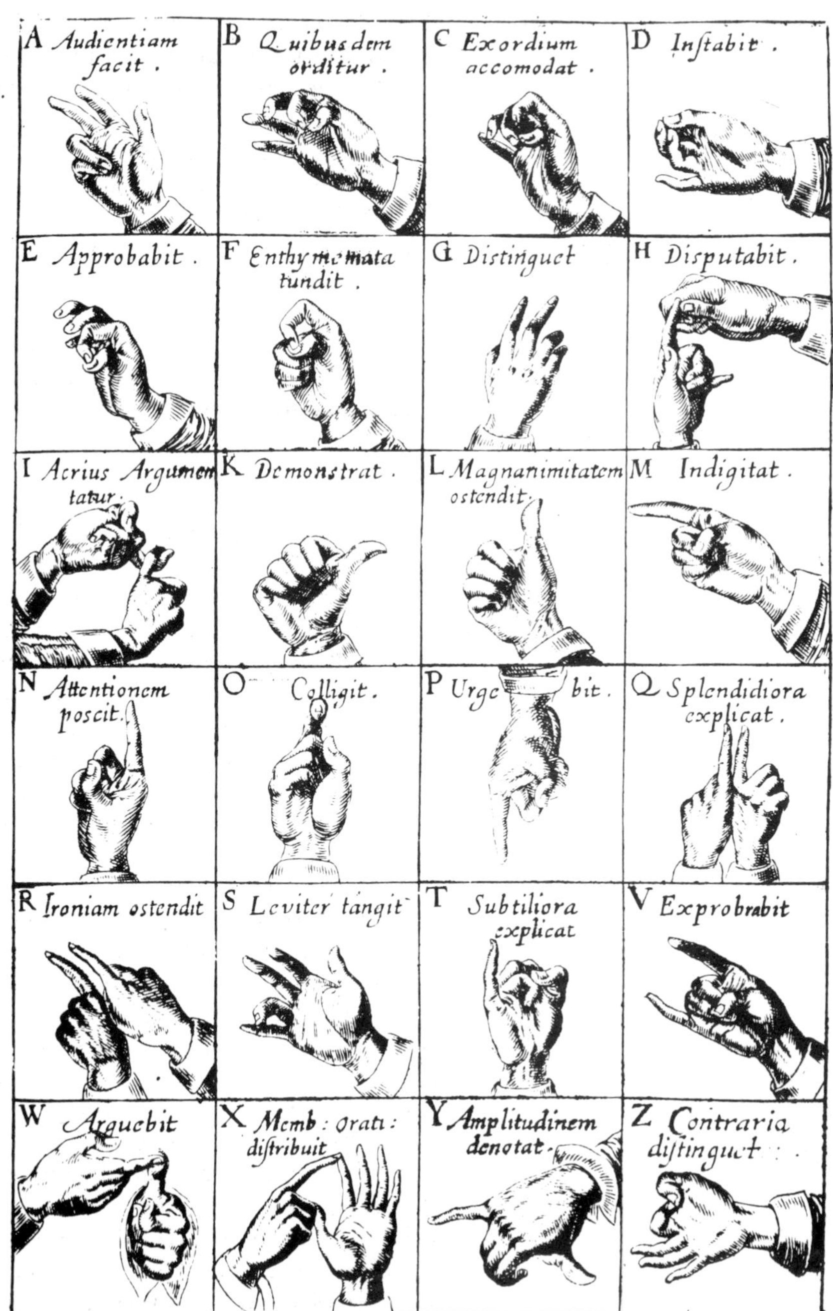

> Downing about it, 'Why,' says [he], 'it is only a little use, and you will understand him and make him understand you, with as much ease as may be'. So I prayed him to tell him that I was afeared that my coach would be gone, and that he should go down and steal one of the seats out of the coach and keep it, and that would make the coachman to stay. He did this, so that the Dumb boy did go down, and like a cunning roague went into the coach, pretending to sleep; and by and by fell to his work, but finds the seats nailed to the coach; so he did all he could, but could not do it; however, stayed there and stayed the coach, till the coachman's patience was quite spent, and beat the Dumb boy with force, and so went away. So the Dumb boy came up and told him all the story, which they below did see all that passed and knew it to be true.

Clearly, the boy's 'strange signs' were not just universal or mime-like, but of the type developed among deaf persons in a community. Equally clearly, they could be learned by hearing people like Downing, who could then serve as an interpreter between English and the boy's sign language, as well as communicating directly. And the 'dumb' boy, like Edward Bone, was able to receive precise instructions and to give detailed information to those familiar with him. So, by the mid-seventeenth century we have ample proof that deaf persons were living active, independent lives based securely on their skill in visual communication and the sign language of their community.

But the seventeenth century was also a time of scientific curiosity and discovery, when trying out new theories was often more important than the final result. Reports from Spain about the work of Ponce de Leon's successors created interest in various forms of communication for deaf people, and Bulwer's book about lipreading was one result. He was obviously unaware that while many deaf people did lipread, for others it was difficult or impossible. Around 1650, theories about the learning of speech and language generally led two different men, later members of the Royal Society for the Improving of Natural Knowledge, to experiment with deaf subjects. The Rev. Dr William Holder, brother-in-law to Christopher Wren, concentrated his efforts on speech teaching. The Rev. Dr John Wallis made use of a manual alphabet for spelling out English words,

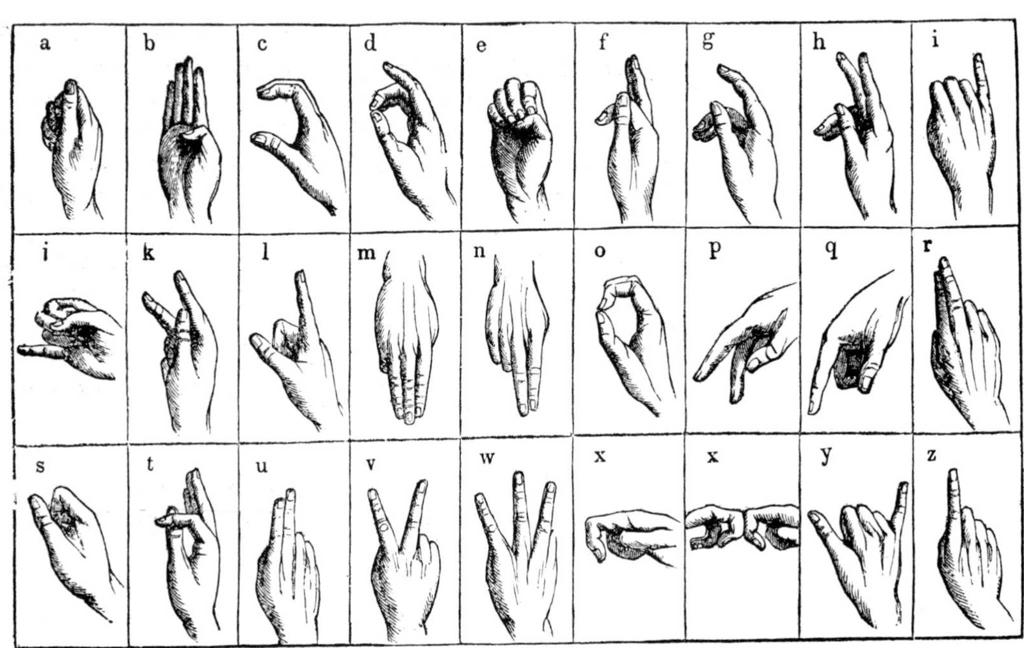

[The Single-handed Alphabet.]

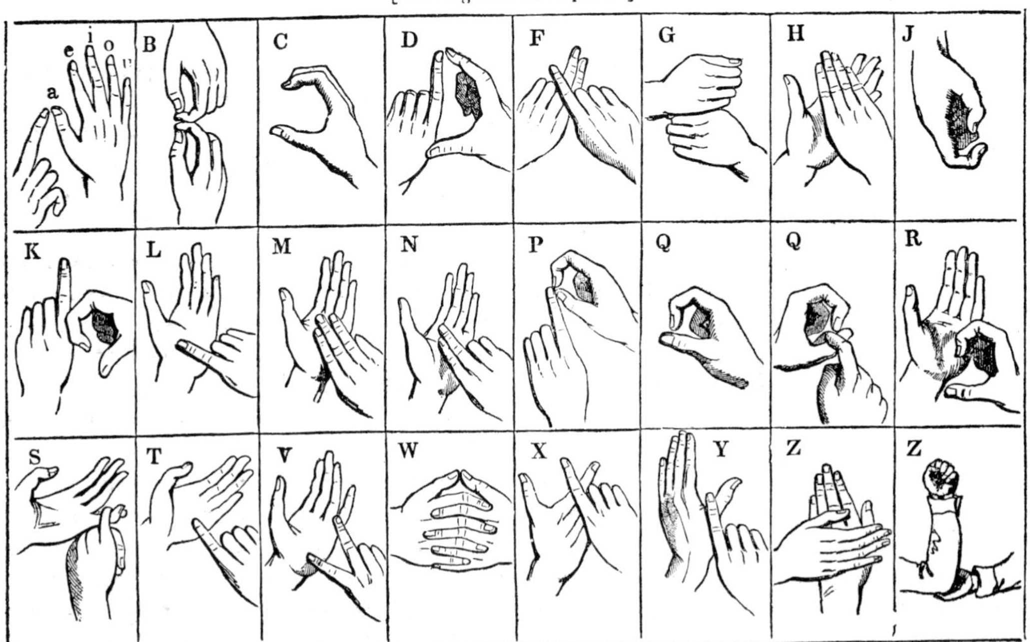

[The Double-handed Alphabet.]

and taught writing as well as speech. Wallis may have taken his one-handed alphabet from that invented in Spain, although both Bulwer and a scholar called George Dalgarno had published versions in Britain. Before this time, there is no record of deaf people using 'fingerspelling', but a two-handed manual alphabet similar to Dalgarno's eventually became a standard resource in BSL.

Experiments along these lines were by then taking place in other European countries besides England, and were supported by fees from the families of the deaf persons concerned. Wealthy families, like those of the Spanish noblemen, were likely to be eager to have their deaf children speak, however crudely or haltingly, since speech was still generally considered proof of intelligence and gentility. From this time on, the occasional and individual successes gained by teachers of speech were considered by hearing people far more noteworthy than the existence of a full sign language within deaf communities.

Eighteenth Century

Britain

By 1760, education of the deaf had become a profitable profession. In that year, a Thomas Braidwood established Britain's first school in Edinburgh, charging the usual high fees for teaching oral and written skills. The school prospered, especially after being visited by Dr Samuel Johnson, who described it enthusiastically in his *Journey to the Western Islands of Scotland* (1775). For the next eighty years or so, Braidwood and his family held a virtual monopoly in the field of deaf education, particularly since he kept his teaching methods secret. From Edinburgh, he later moved to London to set up a new private school, and in 1792 the first 'charity' school was opened in Bermondsey (later moving to the Old Kent Road), under the charge of his nephew, Joseph Watson.

The setting up of schools in different parts of the country from then on contributed to the growth and development of the deaf community. Young deaf people were brought together in one place and formed strong bonds of early friendship. There, the sign language could be standardised from generation to generation so that it spread throughout the community. Braid-

Opposite: Single- and double-handed alphabets as used originally in Britain.

wood never officially gave recognition to the use of sign language, although after his death, his nephew Joseph Watson revealed that 'natural gestures' were included in the Braidwood method. In stressing the learning of a spoken language, and glossing over the existence of a sign language by which the pupils already communicated easily, Braidwood was establishing an educational attitude that was to take firm root in Britain.

France

Across the Channel, in Paris, a man with a very different approach began working with deaf people at about the same time as Braidwood. Charles-Michel, l'Abbé de l'Epée, was an elderly priest who knew nothing about previous educational experiments and theories, even in his own country, when he undertook in the 1760s to give religious instruction to two deaf sisters. Finding that he could not communicate with them by speech or writing, he set himself to learn the signs that they were using. As his work proceeded, he attracted other pupils from among the thriving deaf community of Paris, of which Pierre Desloges was a member. Soon he had sufficient pupils to set up a school, which was the first to be open to all without fee. In time, it was supported as a charity by the King of France, and in 1789 it became the concern of the newly formed National Assembly.

From the beginning, de l'Epée accepted sign language as a true means of communication and as a teaching tool, and he continued to learn it and use it. It never occurred to him to replace it with spoken French, though he did later teach speech where appropriate. His aim was to give his pupils a mastery of French through reading and writing, and for this purpose he developed an elaborate system of 'methodical signs' based on the existing French Sign Language, but including ways of showing every part of French grammar.* Since he also used the pupils' own sign language they now had a means of translating from their sign language into signed French, and back. The school in Paris attracted wide attention under both de l'Epée

Abbé de l'Epée.

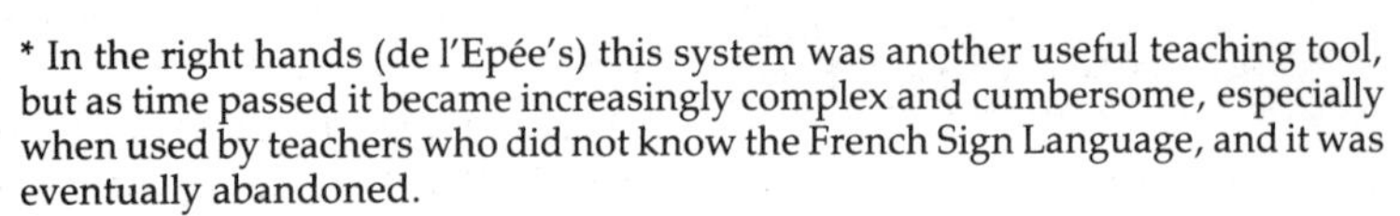

* In the right hands (de l'Epée's) this system was another useful teaching tool, but as time passed it became increasingly complex and cumbersome, especially when used by teachers who did not know the French Sign Language, and it was eventually abandoned.

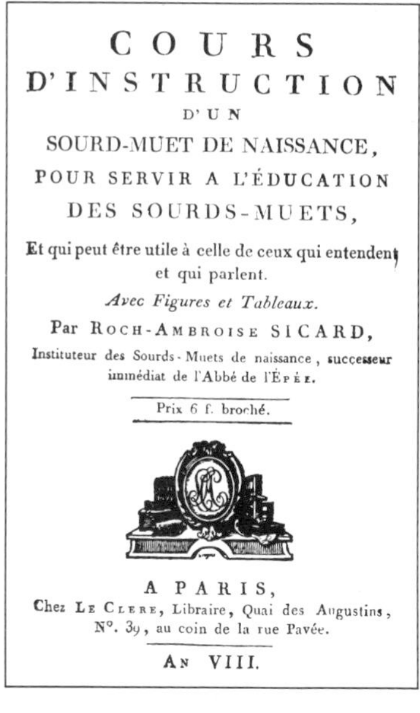

COURS
D'INSTRUCTION
D'UN
SOURD-MUET DE NAISSANCE,
POUR SERVIR A L'ÉDUCATION
DES SOURDS-MUETS,
Et qui peut être utile à celle de ceux qui entendent
et qui parlent.
Avec Figures et Tableaux.
Par ROCH-AMBROISE SICARD,
Instituteur des Sourds-Muets de naissance, successeur
immédiat de l'Abbé de l'Épée.

Prix 6 f. broché.

A PARIS,
Chez LE CLERE, Libraire, Quai des Augustins,
N°. 39, au coin de la rue Pavée.

AN VIII.

The Abbé Sicard and the title page of his book, published in 1800.

and his successor, the Abbé Sicard. Student teachers came from all over Europe and from Russia to learn its methods which were freely passed on (unlike those of Braidwood and other oral teachers). With the steady increase in the number of schools giving instruction through sign language came an even greater increase in the number of literate, knowledgeable deaf men and women, whose professions now included those of teaching assistant, professor and even school director.

Nineteenth Century

An expanding world

In 1816, instruction through sign language spread to the New World. Thomas Gallaudet, a clergyman from Connecticut, came to Europe seeking information about educating deaf persons, and, after being rebuffed by the Braidwoods, found what he needed in Paris. Rather than attempting to learn de l'Epée's methodical signs in the short time he had available, he persuaded one of Sicard's pupil-turned-teachers, Laurent Clerc, to return to Connecticut with him. Clerc, who learned English from Gallaudet during their voyage across the Atlantic, played a

Laurent Clerc.

Thomas Gallaudet and children at the American School for the Deaf in Hartford, Connecticut.

major role in establishing America's first permanent school. He gave talks and demonstrations in sign language to the US President, Members of Congress, and numerous other bodies, in order to raise funds and gain support. He trained Gallaudet and the other new instructors before the school opened, and thereafter was responsible, in addition to his own teaching duties, for training many student teachers who went on to found schools of their own. Like him, several of these founding fathers were deaf.

The many different schools stretching from Russia to the USA, even those that did not use sign language at all, continued to serve as entry points into the deaf community. Within the schools there was comradeship and ease of communication that was cherished for life, and in most there were deaf teachers or principals to look up to, who could describe what life as a deaf adult would be like. And deaf adults themselves, increasingly able not merely to get jobs but to be employed in highly respected occupations, could find in the deaf community that same comradeship and, in time, a marriage partner. The communities became well defined. Regular meeting places were established in many cities, some as an offshoot of a church or mission, and national communities began to emerge. In the second half of the nineteenth century members of these communities included – besides educators – printers, artists, sculptors, scientists, architects, journalists and editors of public newspapers, to name but a few. In the United States many of the leading personalities were graduates of the first college for the deaf, whose charter was signed by Abraham Lincoln in 1864. Its first President was Edward Miner Gallaudet, a non-deaf native signer. He was the son of the Thomas Gallaudet who brought Clerc from France and his deaf wife, Sophia.

By this time, the legal status of non-speaking deaf persons had generally improved, yet there was still much discrimination based on ignorance and prejudice especially against the lower-class and less well educated deaf. But, worse than this, as time went on opposition began to develop against the whole idea of a healthy, flourishing deaf community and its language. Suddenly many people became aware that deaf persons everywhere tended to 'socialise among themselves – to hold reunions, have social gatherings, form their own clubs and associations, publish their own newspapers, hold religious worship . . .'* and so on.

This 'clannishness' disturbed a number of prominent citizens, none more so than a man who believed it could lead to the formation of a deaf variety of the human race. This man, a Scottish-born American whose father had been a teacher of speech in Edinburgh, had himself married a deaf woman. His name was Alexander Graham Bell, and he had recently achieved fame and fortune by almost accidentally inventing the telephone while experimenting with visible speech.

Bell was strongly influenced in his eugenic theories by the research he conducted on Martha's Vineyard, a remote island off the coast of Massachusetts, USA. At that time, the 1880s, most of the inhabitants, deaf or not, could communicate in sign language, because the ratio of deaf people on the island (1:55) was 17·5 times higher than on the mainland (1:2730). The island had been settled in 1640 and by 1680 a group who were descendants of Men of Kent (that is, people from around the Maidstone area) had arrived who had originally emigrated to New England in 1634. By 1870 more than eighty per cent of the population had one ancestor from Kent. Genetically, therefore,

* GANNON, J. *Deaf Heritage* (Washington DC: National Association of the Deaf, 1981).

Professor Alexander Graham Bell.

the Men of Kent descendants were the most probable carriers of the island's inherited deafness.* Martha's Vineyard Sign Language was quite different from the existing American Sign Language on the mainland which suggests that it may have been brought over by the settlers from Kent.

* Maidstone, Kent, was then a centre of a remote and isolated part of the Weald where intermarriage among a restricted population would have produced hereditary deafness. For further discussion of the connection between Maidstone and Martha's Vineyard, see *Everyone Here Spoke Sign Language* by Nora Ellen Groce (Harvard University Press, 1985).

To Bell, any sign language, whatever its origin, was an anathema. He argued for a programme to eradicate deafness by preventing the deaf from marrying, but could not square that with the fact that deaf babies were born to hearing parents and hearing babies to deaf ones on Martha's Vineyard. Unaware of Mendel's genetic theories and unable to fit his findings into his technocratic and eugenic solutions to deafness, he abandoned most of his Martha's Vineyard research unpublished. Ironically, sign language in Martha's Vineyard vanished in the twentieth century when improved communications with the mainland resulted in intermarriage between islanders and new settlers. The subsequent diminishing of the deaf community as the incidence of deafness rapidly declined to the same levels as those of the mainland, meant that hearing islanders no longer had a strong motivation for learning sign language.

Bell believed that the use of sign language in education was what held the deaf community together and that the teaching of speech and lipreading would integrate the deaf into the hearing world. So he put his money and prestige behind the revival of oral teaching that was taking place in Europe and the US towards the end of the nineteenth century.

The aim of 'oralism' was, on the surface, humanitarian: that of 'restoring deaf-mutes to society' through speech and lipreading. The fact that a great many deaf persons had already been restored to society through *education* was, it seems, irrelevant, since these deaf persons did not communicate 'normally'. Speech would 'humanise' them. Oralism, as we have seen, was not a new idea. In some countries, notably Germany, oral theories had predominated from the beginning, although deaf Germans still used German Sign Language. But now, with the support of powerful men like Bell, the new oralists became fanatical in their efforts to eliminate sign language from education. It was not enough that this should happen in one classroom, or one school, or even one country: it had to be world-wide. In 1878, for the first time, an international congress of those concerned in the education of the deaf was held in Paris. It attracted only twenty-seven teachers, mainly European supporters of oralism, who thus had an opportunity to link up and confer. Two years later, in 1880, the Second Congress took place in Milan, Italy. Like the previous one, it could hardly be called international. Of the 164 participants, eighty-seven were

Italian, fifty-six French, eight English and five American, with eight from other nations. The programme of the Congress and the way it was governed allowed little discussion to take place. On the final day, the Congress voted overwhelmingly in favour of a resolution that in teaching the deaf 'the pure oral method ought to be preferred'. Only the five Americans, there on behalf of fifty-one schools and over 6000 pupils who used American Sign Language, voted against the resolution, but the rule was one man, one vote.

The resolutions of this 'Kangaroo Congress' had far-reaching implications in the lives of deaf people. They were made at the time when technological developments such as those of Bell seemed to promise unlimited progress, including the elimination of deafness and other imperfections of mankind. Such a goal fitted in with popular theories relating to 'the perfect race' and to the supremacy of certain languages (for example, English as opposed to Welsh, Gaelic and other minority languages). Not only were wealth, prestige and intellectual theories on the side of the oralists, but the parents of deaf children were again easily recruited to the cause by the hope that it would make their children 'normal'. Governing bodies were thus increasingly persuaded to enforce oralism in schools, against the protests of the deaf community.

In Britain, as the twentieth century got under way British Sign Language gradually disappeared from the classrooms. Along with it went deaf teachers, who were considered unable to teach by speech and lipreading. The schools began to turn out 'oral successes', usually partially-deaf and deafened children, with some born deaf of deaf parents or with middle or upper-class backgrounds. They also turned out 'oral failures' across the whole range. Most children continued to use BSL throughout their school days, often in the face of punishment, but by the time they left school the 'successes' were using a blend of signs and English*, and looking down on the 'failures', who were still using BSL. The latter, because they could no longer get information and instruction in their own language, and because the world was becoming a more literate and sound-dependent one, could no longer compete in education or employment. They accepted an inferior status once again.

* Now known as Signs Supporting English – see Glossary (p. 111).

2
THE MODERN DEAF COMMUNITY

by Paddy Ladd

British Sign Language in the deaf community had reached a peak around the time of the Milan Conference in 1880. But once governments, working with oralists, set in motion their programmes to eradicate it, it was a hundred years before the language and its people started to emerge with confidence again. During this time, the fate of BSL and its users was determined by four factors:

1 The policies of the education system in the United Kingdom.
2 The response of the official deaf organisations.
3 The response of the community itself.
4 The role of the welfare officers for the community.

1 Education Policies

British Sign Language has been affected more severely by education policies than almost any other minority language, because it is not passed down primarily from generation to generation. Ninety per cent of deaf children have hearing parents, and ninety per cent of deaf marriages produce hearing children. In addition, the deaf community does not live in close-knit geographical areas. Instead the main source for the language's growth and development has been in the residential schools, where deaf children have been educated from the eighteenth century onward. Throughout the twentieth century the oralists have brought about a succession of changes in deaf education. These include:

a) The suppression of sign language as a means of instruction and communication in the deaf schools.
b) Removal of deaf teachers. Deaf teachers were seen as subversive influences on deaf children in that they continued to use

BSL, and by the First World War virtually all had been removed from their posts.

c) The setting up of day schools. Once BSL had been banned in the classroom, the only place left for it was out-of-school hours. As the number of day schools grew, and more children went home at 4 o'clock to families who could barely communicate with them, a large part of the time needed to develop the language and to enjoy deaf culture positively was taken away.

d) The enforcement of stricter measures out of school. Attempts to remove BSL from the playgrounds and dormitories of the residential schools became more strenuous. The language was driven almost into the toilets by a variety of methods, ranging from physical chastisement to setting children to spy on each other. Pupils often had to set up someone to keep watch for the teachers whilst they grabbed stolen minutes to sign with each other.

e) Selection at Eleven Plus. After the Second World War, a grammar school for the deaf was established in the south of England. In any community, the 'intelligentsia' play a major role in shaping its destiny. So, by bringing together many of the brightest deaf in the United Kingdom and subjecting them to an intensely oral regime, oralists were able in effect to behead the British deaf population. Pupils of the school were instilled with a feeling of superiority over other deaf people, because they did not need to 'descend' to BSL, and they were exhorted not to mix with the community as adults. The success of this programming can be seen from one informal survey in Scotland, which showed that out of 144 ex-pupils of that school, only six were known to belong to the deaf community.

The contrast with the American situation was enormous, for the survival of American Sign Language was made easier by its continued use in Gallaudet College, the focus of higher aspirations for deaf Americans.

f) The spread of personal hearing aids after 1945. This made it possible to halve the deaf community in the space of a few years. It separated out the partially deaf, previously educated in deaf schools, who were moved into schools of their own or units in hearing schools (Partially Hearing Units (PHUs) – see Glossary, p. 110) where BSL had no roots.

g) Parental guidance. After the Second World War, health, educational and social services were consolidated and these all directed parental guidance towards oral policies. This, together with the setting up of the National Deaf Children's Society by orally influenced parents, meant that there was no escape from anti-BSL philosophies. The stranglehold on the development of the British deaf community seemed complete.

During the 1970s, however, concern about the standards of deaf education could no longer be suppressed. But it was not until 1979 that the first ever comprehensive deaf school leavers survey* revealed the sorry truth. Their reading age averaged 8·75 years, their speech was mostly unintelligible and their lipreading no better than a hearing child with no practice. Oralism's failures were finally exposed. The scene was set for change.

2 *The Organised Deaf Response*

Deaf communities all over the world were jolted by the Milan Conference, and started to set up their own national organisations as a result. In Britain, the British Deaf and Dumb Association was formed in 1890, and at its first conference the following resolution was passed: 'This Congress . . . indignantly protests against the imputation that the finger and sign language is barbarous. We consider such a mode of exchanging our ideas as most natural and indispensable, and that the combined system of education (i.e. a blend of signs and English) is by far preferable to the so-called Pure Oral.'

But when at the Paris Conference of 1900 deaf teachers, who were in the majority, were prevented from participating, it was clear that the last major deaf lobby had failed. So, as the oralists began to implement their programmes with government backing, The British Deaf and Dumb Association (it became the British Deaf Association (BDA) in 1961) turned its energies towards keeping the national community together. They organised their own social, welfare and educational facilities, and although successive conferences passed resolutions echoing the one above, it was to no avail. Gradually the view that The British Deaf and Dumb Association was only a social group became entrenched.

As oralism tightened its grip and deaf literacy in English declined, the organisation became dominated mainly by hear-

* CONRAD, R. *The Deaf School Child* (Harper & Row, London, 1979).

ing people, so that by the 1970s deaf involvement at the top was almost nil. Although the BDA had by then over 100 branches, many were dominated by people who looked down on British Sign Language, and this effectively blocked the grass-roots users of BSL from participation. Nevertheless, without the BDA and its social activities, the backbone of the deaf community would have been broken, and it was the existence of that structure that helped to start its revival in the 1980s.

3 *The Deaf Community's Response*

Deaf clubs

By 1880, there was a strong network of deaf clubs (then called missions) in major towns throughout the United Kingdom, which were often set up by deaf people who had raised the money to buy the buildings. By the end of the century, this growth had spread to the smaller towns, and thus British Sign Language flourished nationally in the adult community.

In many clubs, educational activities took place. Speakers gave lectures interpreted in BSL, and the level of debate was reportedly high; signed drama was also popular. As yet, there was no attempt to stop school leavers from joining the clubs, so continuity was maintained and the language was passed on to young people.

As the twentieth century moved on, however, there were fewer school leavers who could communicate effectively in either English or British Sign Language thanks to the emphasis on oral teaching. Young people entering deaf clubs could not understand or be understood by the existing members. Few of them were interested in or capable of holding key posts in the club, such as secretary or treasurer. In fact, because English was used for club reports and correspondence, most of these posts came to be held by bilinguals, and these people came to consider Signs Supporting English (see Glossary, p. 111) to be superior to BSL – an attitude which often caused a rift between officials and club members. Despite this, however, the clubs were and are crucial to the community in keeping it together.

Many clubs have set up youth sections which attract young deaf who have been placed in PHUs or hearing schools and who thus belatedly find their base in the deaf community. The task of locating such young people is made difficult by the opposition put up by some parents and oral teachers. Most deaf clubs also have long-established sports sections, which, through inter-club competitions, provide the opportunity for members to travel throughout Britain. What is more, unlike with hearing amateur sports fixtures where usually just the team travels, a good proportion of a deaf club will move from one town to another for these events, and regional and national social contacts – and thus BSL itself – are maintained.

Deaf publications

The response of deaf publications at the time of the first oralist attack was to re-affirm conscious pride in British Sign Language and deaf culture. Even though the magazines were of necessity written in English, they took a major role in opposing the suppression of BSL. If one looks through the pages of *The British Deaf-Mute*, and its successors (published between 1892 and 1955), one continually finds examples ranging from humour to anger concerning the attempts to enforce an oralist approach to teaching deaf children in Britain. In one early issue the following newspaper report concerning a deaf school in Germany was reprinted:

> An action for slander brought by the director and masters of the Deaf-mute Institute at Weissenfels on the Saale against Doctor Heidsieck, a teacher of deaf-mutes in this city, who in a pamphlet published here, accused these officials of being guilty of practising various forms of cruelty upon their deaf-mute pupils, has been concluded here. The evidence given during the trial revealed the fact that the directors and masters at the Institute had been in the habit of practising disgraceful cruelties upon the children while instructing them in the use of oral language. It transpired that in the classes when this form of teaching was given the pupils had their hands tied behind their backs so as to prevent them from conversing by signs, and that they were moreover continually flogged with canes and struck with rulers. On one occasion twelve of them came out of the class covered with blood.
>
> The teachers, in endeavouring to induce their pupils to pronounce sibilants, had forced instruments into their

THE ASSOCIATION OF MISSIONARIES *versus* THE BRITISH DEAF AND DUMB ASSOCIATION.

(Cartoon from 'The British Deaf-Mute')

mouths which made the tongue bleed, and in order to make the children open their mouths the masters pinched their noses so hard as to cause blood to flow. Moreover, both directors and masters were accused of striking the pupils indiscriminately with their fists.

Little by little the public are becoming enlightened upon this much vaunted German system, which Mr St Ackers and other benevolent visionaries have been trying so hard to foist on us in England. Dr Heidsieck's pamphlet was one of the first things that opened people's eyes. Then came the

> petition of the 800 educated deaf-mutes to the Emperor against the oral system, and now comes this crowning disgrace at Weissenfels. . . .
>
> It will now be in order to institute a prosecution of the Director and Masters of Weissenfels for the abominable cruelties of which they have been guilty. We should like to know what steps the Public Prosecutor intends to take, and sincerely hope that exemplary punishment will be inflicted, not for vengeance sake, but because while the oral system continues to be the Government system of Germany, such punishments are necessary if the schools are not to be turned into torture chambers.

In spite of the campaigning efforts of deaf magazines, as the twentieth century progressed, fewer deaf people were able to read English and fewer still able to write it. This decline in English literacy continued to the extent that, in the late 1960s, the BDA had to take over publication of the magazine that had formerly been the voice of the deaf community and which became instead almost entirely written and edited by hearing people until its resurgence in the 1980s.

4 *The Rise of Welfare Services*

Most deaf clubs were started by deaf people themselves, but during the later part of the nineteenth century, more and more hearing people were brought in to minister to the members' spiritual needs. This evolved into a profession of its own, missioners to the deaf, who were mostly hearing members of the BSL community with deaf parents and relatives.

Their work began to increase in scope. It involved finding jobs for school leavers, interpreting from English into British Sign Language in a wide range of settings, and dealing with welfare problems. Indeed, this meant that they officially became Welfare Officers to the Deaf as time went on, and more deaf people lost confidence in their ability to solve the problems an oralist education had omitted to prepare them for. By the 1950s, many Welfare Officers to the Deaf were running the deaf clubs themselves, acting as self-appointed representatives from the club to the management committee, made up for the most part of local hearing notables who knew nothing about the deaf.

Thus they gradually became benevolent despots in their local deaf community.

So, over a period of generations the missioner passed from being an ally to being an active agent in keeping deaf people 'in their place'. When these same people took over the running of the British Deaf and Dumb Association, would-be deaf activists found themselves shut out on all sides. Despite this, the Welfare Officer to the Deaf was still valued as a member of the community. This has as much to do with their sharing a common language, British Sign Language, as with the fact that they often had deaf relatives. Indeed, many of the earlier missioners took great pride in their aesthetic use of BSL, and some of them – for example, the Reverend Gilby – would attract enormous attendances for their sermons and lectures chiefly for their beautiful use of British Sign Language.

But even this language-using bond was broken. As local government started to take over and run welfare services for the population as a whole, so too did a new kind of welfare service emerge to deal with the deaf community. This service, although it produced workers who were in many cases more 'enlightened' and more encouraging than the former Welfare Officers to the Deaf, largely failed to recognise that deaf people formed a linguistic community, and thought that 'learning to communicate with the deaf' was enough. This and other factors led to an actual fall in numbers of those who had a good command of British Sign Language, and many deaf people came to regret the passing of the Welfare Officers to the Deaf, despite their autocratic behaviour. Thus the deaf community lost the potential support for British Sign Language from the only group of hearing people who were aware of it.

The British Sign Language Community Today

Given all the foregoing history, one may wonder how there is any community left in Britain. But British Sign Language has perhaps one advantage over the other languages that have been stamped out over the centuries – its users have no other reasonable means of communication. What's more, after growing up and joining their local club, few continue to take the oralists seriously. Their spirit of defiance is, in many cases very strong:

> 'You can cut off the fingers of deaf people and they will sign with their arms. And you can cut off their arms and they will sign with their shoulders'.
>
> (quoted in J. G. Furth *Thinking without Language*, 1973, p. 34)

In addition, the community has a very firm core. The ten per cent who have deaf parents, are brought up with BSL as a first language at home and have a life in the deaf clubs and community from babyhood, are themselves living proof that there is a British Sign Language community. Some can trace their deaf ancestors back seven generations, to the late 1700s. The extra confidence which is inbuilt, together with a much higher degree of English literacy than those with hearing parents, has meant that, in many areas, these people held the community together, although their worth has been highly underestimated by both the oralist education system and society in general.

Another group who played a crucial part in keeping the community alive were those who were deafened in childhood after already learning English. Many became bilingual and their work and advocacy within the community helped it from folding through lack of sufficient literacy to keep the clubs running, to give but one example.

So the community still survives, despite the heavy damage inflicted over the last hundred years, and club life is still its hub.

How can one describe the community's life in dry statistics and data? But, come to that, how can one describe it in words? Perhaps the life, bustle and laughter when deaf people get together and have the chance to use their language in full flow is best left to the imagination. Notable scenes in deaf culture include the standing joke of the club committee trying to push people out at closing time, and crowds standing around in the street signing for a good hour afterwards. Or of people of all ages staying up half the night together, telling jokes and stories (a major part of deaf culture), signing songs or poems or playing sign language-based games. Or of a regional rally, where a town centre is taken over by sign language for a weekend, and people from all over the country greet old schoolfriends across the street on their morning promenade.

At present there are over 200 clubs throughout the United Kingdom, and a survey of one such club revealed that fifty-eight per cent of the members attended at least weekly (seventy per cent of the men and forty-eight per cent of women). The rest of the time, unless one has a deaf spouse, is spent effectively in the hearing, English-speaking world which builds up a steady pressure that simply has to find release in being with other British Sign Language users. In addition, there is a strong national identity, as many people keep up old school contacts and, in so doing, make many others, which in turn are maintained. One classic example is the way news travels around the community. Information can go from one end of the country to the other and back again in a matter of days, despite the lack of access to the telephone.

In many cases there is an international consciousness too. It is much easier for signers from different countries to grasp and adapt to each others' visual messages, than for two speakers to create a common tongue. There is considerable international traffic between the different deaf communities, with individuals launching themselves into foreign lands and banking on making deaf contacts to make the trips successful.

Hearing members of the deaf community

Many people are surprised to learn that hearing people can be part of the British Sign Language community. But if one realises that hearing children of deaf parents will often have BSL as their first language and English as their second, it begins to make sense. For many, deaf-club life is part of their Saturday night childhood, whether or not they stay members and work in deaf-related occupations as adults. In addition, deaf people have hearing brothers and sisters and, as the teaching of British Sign Language spreads, one can anticipate an increase in the number of siblings, as well as parents and workmates, who will learn the language enough to take part in the community.

Sign language variation within the community

The deaf community can be recognised as a minority group. Since BSL has now been identified as a distinct language in use within that community, it follows that those who use it form one of Britain's language minorities. As in these other minorities, the influence of the surrounding dominant language, i.e. English, is always felt. Some members will be bilingual (know both languages equally well). Others will be more fluent in one language than in the other. As they interact with each other and with members of the English-speaking majority, the result is often the creation of pidgin forms of communication, which borrow from each language.

In the deaf community the same effect occurs, to the confusion of the interested newcomer. There are two overall pidgin forms, one closer to English and one to BSL. These have been described by several researchers as Pidgin Sign English (PSE) and Pidgin Sign Language (PSL). PSE includes a variation already mentioned that has been given a name of its own, Signs Supporting English. In PSE the signs of BSL are used mainly to reinforce the information given by voiced or silent English speech and fingerspelled words, and comparatively few of the visual/spatial features of BSL grammar are present. This approximate representation of English is used chiefly by those members of the community, both hearing and deaf, whose first language is English rather than BSL, and by non-members who learn 'to sign' in order to communicate with deaf people.

In contrast, Pidgin Sign Language relies heavily on BSL for sign vocabulary and grammar, but is still influenced to some extent by English. This can be seen in the varying use of English lip patterns, fingerspelled words and sign order. Individuals who are fluent in BSL but less so in English will usually shift into this pidgin form when in contact with English speakers or users of SSE.

Outside the community, attempts have been made to develop forms of a signing that will render English into a fully visible form for educational purposes. These include Signed English and the Paget-Gorman Sign System (see Glossary).

Deaf Culture, Art and History

All languages develop creative forms, using metaphors, puns, symbols and so on, both to express new ideas, which in turn get built on and developed further, and also through simply playing with the language. If a language is severely oppressed, however, these creative forms can be lost, and it can contract down to a very functional level, simply serving everyday needs.

Something similar has happened to British Sign Language during this century. New signs are still developed, but it is only recently that the upturn in pride in the language has started to

produce signs which express new ideas as a result of playing with old ones.

There are a number of ways in which the community currently expresses itself artistically. The one most taken for granted, storytelling, is in fact the one which has survived best. Drama is popular, but as yet has little to do with reflecting deaf people's language and culture. The other three, signed poetry, signed songs and cabaret, have only just started to develop again, but if recent American experience is anything to go by, they could become crucial not only in restoring deaf pride, but in capturing the attention of the hearing public.

Another result of the oppression of a linguistic group is that its history is erased, and this has especially been the case with British Sign Language, where oralist policies have tried to emphasise that each deaf child is a unique and isolated 'non-hearing' child. So the very concept of history in the deaf community has all but disappeared and deaf cultural activities have consequently lost the crucial sense of historical self-awareness and perspective that a language community needs to be fully alive. One deaf person who has fought a lone battle in this century to maintain historical pride is Arthur Dimmock. For forty-two years, he has published regular columns of news from abroad and home, and stories about deaf people past and present in deaf publications around the world. In his style he is clearly the last link between the deaf consciousness that produced *The British Deaf-Mute* and the present day.

Arthur Dimmock.

Recently there have been signs of an awakened interest in the true deaf history, provoked by the publication of Harlan Lane's book, *When the Mind Hears*, an account of events in France and America from 1750–1900, which makes it clear that the history of deaf people is inescapably the history of their language and its oppression.

The British Sign Language Community and the Technological Age

Right up to the 1920s, deaf people could function at roughly the same level as the hearing world. Employment using trade skills was more common than office skills. There were few telephones, no radio, no television, and films were still silent. At a film show deaf people could sit in a hearing audience and come out equal at the end. Indeed a number of deaf people had significant parts in the old silent movie world, some of them influencing Charlie Chaplin himself.

Once these technological devices caught on and speeded up the modern world, however, deaf people were pushed aside. No attempt was made to adapt technology for their use, apart from hearing aids. The telephone in particular has been used as an excuse to keep deaf people out of white collar jobs.

At last there are some belated moves to adapt technology to the needs of deaf people. Small, portable teletypewriters have started to come onto the market, which give deaf people the ability to communicate over unlimited distances within Britain. However, these can only be used to call people who also own a machine, of course, and will not become as widely used in Britain as elsewhere until:

a) The quality of the machines improves;
b) Public services and businesses purchase them;
c) Switchboards which can link them with voice 'phones are widely developed;
d) Deaf persons' literacy in English improves.

Some developments are taking place to link teletypewriters with data-base mailboxes and computer terminals, and if this caught on, deaf people would at last have something like equality of provision in the field of information technology.

In the last few years, serious steps have been taken by television companies to provide a better service to deaf viewers. A growing percentage of programmes are now close-captioned, i.e. subtitled via Ceefax or Oracle, who also provide deaf magazine pages. In addition, most channels have started to provide token television programming in British Sign Language and to place interpreters on local television news. The advent of video has meant that the perfect form for transmission of information in BSL has arrived. In other countries this has meant that deaf people can make their own magazine programmes and even their own 'video-letters' to send to friends. Video also offers a solution to the problem of illiteracy in English, as written information from local and central authorities can be translated on to videotape, thus giving deaf people long overdue access to public information. In Britain, however, lack of funds and lack of Government interest is likely to hold up this much-needed development.

The Deaf Revival

In the past ten years, there has been a revival in the strength of the British Sign Language community, which has taken several forms. In 1976, a number of deaf people, impatient with the lack of self-advocacy, formed the National Union of the Deaf (NUD). Although this organisation has remained small, it has provided the impetus for deaf people once again to take charge of their own affairs, and has significantly influenced a number of important trends.

In 1974, the British Deaf Association started to speak out more vociferously for sign language, and in 1981 became more of an active campaigning body than before. In 1982 they produced a manifesto asking for official recognition of British Sign Language as a native British language, and made clear to the hearing world deaf people's aspirations to greater equality. In 1983, the first ever major lobby of the House of Commons took place, and in 1985, in conjunction with the National Union of the Deaf, a series of campaigns took place at the international Conference of Education of the Deaf in Manchester which formed the most successful fightback seen this century.

Inspired by developments in America, and encouraged by the advocacy of the organisations above, several schools have reverted back to using sign language in the classroom. These changes started with Signed English, but British Sign Language itself is beginning to find acceptance once more. The previous climate of fear is beginning to be replaced by one of happy co-operation between parents, teachers and the deaf community. However, there are few indications that deaf people are being encouraged to train as teachers, although more are now being accepted as classroom assistants in schools.

Sign language research

Few things changed people's thinking on this issue so radically and so fast as sign language research. Inspired by William Stokoe's work on American Sign Language, teams in Edinburgh and Bristol examined British Sign Language and found it was indeed a language, and one of greater complexity than had ever been suspected. By simply declaring that British Sign Language *was* a language, people's conceptions changed. Deaf people officially had something positive and attractive which made them equal to hearing people; deafness was not just viewed as being about the *loss* of something. And the difference in the way hearing people perceived deaf people's intelligence and ability can be measured by considering what must have been the previous image held – that signs were just monkey gestures used by a group of sub-humans who did not even have a language. Indeed the change has immense potential, for now the deaf community has a way of measuring the degree of respect they are or are not getting from society, by the degree to which it accepts their means of communication. Now the developing philosophy is 'Accept me – accept my language'.

In 1983, the Swedish government officially recognised Swedish Sign Language as a native language of Sweden. This has set a crucial world precedent, a goal for other deaf communities to strive for in order to achieve political recognition as a distinct sociocultural group rather than as a scattering of disabled individuals requiring state charity.

Other changes that have resulted from the linguistic recognition of BSL include:

i) The deaf community can now be identified as a linguistic minority, rather than as individual handicapped people whose problem is the inability to hear sounds, and who are themselves a problem. This has made the issue a question of discrimination against a language-using group, and society's attitude has become the problem. Indeed, there is an ongoing National Union of the Deaf campaign, led by the current secretary, Raymond Lee, to get the United Nations to place sign languages under the protection of rulings on linguistic minorities (and thus prevent the abuses of oralism from re-occurring).

ii) Inadequacies of teaching and interpreting methods have become much easier to identify now that British Sign Language is seen as a bona fide language, and we can look forward to an era of improved professional standards.

iii) Greater prominence has been given to grass-roots British Sign Language users, especially the deaf of deaf parents, rather than the previous models, who were people with good oral or English skills, and who were usually deafened people whose commitment to the deaf world was often equivocal.

iv) Although welfare work had always included interpreting, little attention had previously been given to the subject. Once British Sign Language was formally acknowledged, and deaf people began to take more of an active role in their own and society's affairs, the demand for interpreters mushroomed, and whole areas of previous neglect came to light. These included the absence of interpreters in higher education, in the workplace, at social functions and so on. Although there are still far too few interpreters, and most of the work is still done almost on an *ad hoc* basis, we seem to be entering an age where this will become a major profession. It has been interesting to note that once an interpreter is present at a meeting of hearing people, interest in the deaf suddenly shoots up, and a host of issues emerge. It is interesting also to speculate how much more prominent in the public eye deaf people would have become, but for oralist policies driving British Sign Language underground. More sobering is the realisation that the developments described above have come just in time, for in recent years there have been further changes in educational policy that, if unopposed, could bring the deaf community close to extinction.

The Oralist Responses

Oralist policies continue to place deaf children into hearing schools, either in groups in Partially Hearing Units, or alone in 'individualised integration'. These moves, backed by the Warnock Report and the 1981 Education Act, have resulted in deaf schools all over the country being closed, including some which had started to use sign language. So far has this gone that the Department of Education and Science no longer even recognises that there is such a thing as a category of 'deaf children' placing them instead into the category 'Children with special needs'. Encouraged by this, local authorities have started to cut expenditure on deaf education, the irony being that if *proper* integration programmes with interpreters etc. were set up, it would actually be *more* expensive than deaf school education.

In the early 1980s, medical people started to devise cochlear implant surgery, which, although highly experimental in nature, has been performed on many deaf children in America and Europe. The media, ready as ever to treat deafness in science-fiction terms, gave these operations massive publicity, creating false hopes in parents and deaf teenagers alike. Once again, the oralist idea of 'getting rid of deafness' has been put back on the agenda, and the recent improvements of deaf life are once again facing severe threats.

The Media and the BSL Community

Once the deaf community had been driven underground, hearing people's images of deafness had to be obtained from the media. The latter insist upon seeing deafness in terms of something that can be 'overcome', and give prominence to a select few oral deaf people who succeed in behaving like hearing people by, for example, playing musical instruments, ballet dancing, having cochlear implants, and so on. Interestingly, this was the case right back at the beginning of oralism, when even *The Times* had declared that 'Deafness is abolished'.

In 1976, however, the National Union of the Deaf, recognising that the key to the community's survival was in being seen on television, began to campaign for regular programmes in BSL. A pilot programme was made in 1979 for BBC Television's *Open Door*, aptly named *Signs of Life*, and a joint campaign thereafter with the British Deaf Association, called the Deaf Broadcasting Campaign, resulted in the establishment of the magazine programme *See Hear* in 1981. This has been followed by programmes on ITV and Channel 4, through which the image and status of British Sign Language users and their community has grown apace.

Despite the media influence of oral deaf models, there has nevertheless remained in the general public a fascination for sign language, one that we can trace right back in history, as was mentioned at the beginning of this chapter. This came together with the spread of BSL in the media in the 1980s, to produce a new peak, a televised teaching series *British Sign Language*.

In the final analysis then, in a future where the struggle for survival of the British Sign Language community has intensified on both sides, the readers of this book, with their committed interest in the language and its people are in an interesting position. For the first time, the hearing public on a wide scale are active participants in the struggle for final recognition or obliteration of the deaf community and British Sign Language.

GUIDE TO CHAPTER 3

1 Illustrations

The photographs and drawings in this book can only give the reader some idea about how a sign is made. Arrows cannot precisely reproduce hand movements, while many shots would be needed to show changes in posture or expression. Students should therefore check usage with a local teacher or user of BSL wherever possible.

2 Explanations

Since BSL has no written form, signs are usually represented by English words or *glosses*, e.g. RUN. This can be misleading, because the English word 'run' has many meanings, but RUN refers only to the physical act of running

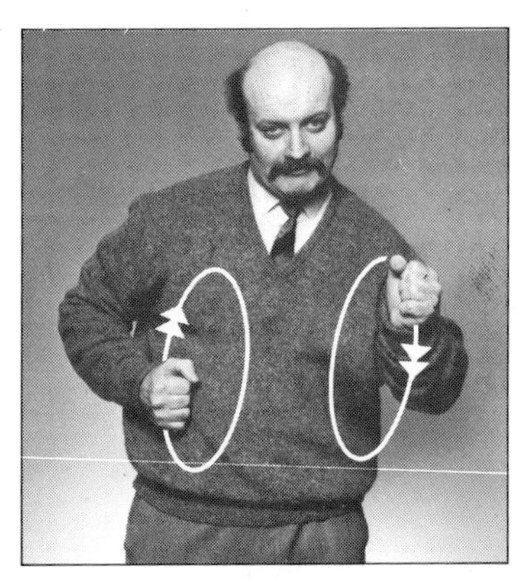

RUN

(RUN-A-TAP)

(RUN-A-MEETING)

On the other hand one sign may have to be glossed by several English words, e.g. A-FORTNIGHT-AGO. The system used in this book is as follows:

a) The English translation of a sign is given in inverted commas and in a different type, e.g. 'Open the drawer'.

b) Glosses are written in capital letters also in the different typeface, e.g. RUN.

c) Where one sign needs to be glossed by several English words, the words are joined by hyphens, e.g. EVERY-YEAR, CHATTING-TO-EACH-OTHER.

d) Words or phrases printed in small letters show meaning that is not given on the hands. In the phrase LOOK-AT-(HIM)-with-surprise, the sign LOOK-AT is accompanied by information on the face meaning 'with surprise' which is part of the full message.

e) Brackets are added when the writer gives some information that could be changed. The sign LOOK-AT could be directed at any person or thing, so it might be LOOK-AT-(HER) or (IT), and so on. Brackets are also put round text which comments on the way a sign is used or made, but which is not a gloss or translation.

Symbols used to describe movements

Closed arrow – movement *across* the body (side to side or up and down)

Open arrow – movement *away from* or *towards* the body

Open hand closing (or thumb and finger closing)

Closed hand opening

Slow movement

Fast movement

'Tapping'

'Crumbling' (between fingertips and thumb)

Fist

Finger movements

Movement repeated (backwards/forwards or side to side)

'Stop' indicates sudden finish to movement

Repeated movement (usually small short movement)

Both hands move together

Usually, hand associated moves in circular motion in direction of arrow

Both hands move simultaneously in circular motion – one following the other

Slight movement

3
HOW THE LANGUAGE WORKS

Sign language is visual

All human languages are produced by the body. Spoken languages are used among people who can hear their own and others' voices, and depend on sound for making and sending their messages. The parts of the body used for speech include the lungs, vocal cords, tongue and lips. Messages carried by sound waves are received by the ear and interpreted by the brain. When all the links in this complex chain are working, spoken communication is a natural and effortless process.

Sign languages are equally complex and achieve communication just as naturally and easily, but they are used among people who cannot hear. Instead of sound, the message carrier is vision. Unlike a speaker, whose lips make the only visible movement, a signer uses parts of the body that can be seen: the hands and arms, the face, head and upper body. Movements of these parts convey messages to the receiver's eyes and brain. Since these movements are visible and physical, the signer in flow is a lively, mobile figure.

It can be expected that a language based on vision will work very differently from one based on sound. Indeed, this difference has confused many people who have had contact with sign language over the past hundred years. Looking for sound-based structures they have dismissed sign language as 'mere random gestures, imitative and transparent in meaning, a crude and primitive communication system, unlike real language'.* This attitude has changed in the past twenty-five years as a result of linguistic studies, increasingly aided by the availability of a cheap means of making visual records for analysis –

A full bibliography detailing all source material used in the preparation of this chapter is available from the address on page 129.

* Quoted by Michael Stubbs in *British Sign Language* by M. Deuchar (Routledge & Kegan Paul, 1984).

the videotape. This invention has enabled linguists to study exactly how a signer sends his messages, and to demonstrate that this way of communication is rightly called a language.

Not all visual communication is language

Sign languages have in the past been dismissed as mere gesture, or classed with mime. This confusion has arisen because all three share the same channel of communication – vision – and at times express themselves through similar movements of the body. But gesture and mime are not languages, as can be seen.

a) Gestures are only occasionally used on their own to give brief messages, usually in situations where hearing is difficult. More often they are used to reinforce the meaning of speech. Each speaker, if he uses gestures at all, uses them differently. They are not standard or precise, but are personal to the speaker. Signers and speakers do share certain natural gestures derived from common experience, e.g. pointing up and down, nodding, head-shaking, similar facial expressions for doubt or surprise. But signers use these gestures with other signs in ways that give consistent and precise meanings or shades of meaning when linked together, and this meaning is independent of spoken language.

b) Mime is an art form, not a language. A mime artist imitates life, using his own set of conventional gestures, facial expressions and movements. He tells his story by acting it out in real time, in the present, and moves around freely in the space provided. But the signer, like a speaker, can refer to the past, present or future. He remains in one place while he sends his message, using only the space around himself as a stage for his story. Some of his actions may seem like mime, but even these fit into grammatical patterns that carry precise meanings. When signers need to communicate with hearing people they often emphasise the mime elements of their language to find a common ground. This may have led to the original confusion between sign and mime.

Sign language is not international

Many people ask if the same sign language is used all over the world. But just as each nation has its own spoken language, so each national deaf community has its own sign language, developed over centuries. The first sign language to be studied by linguists, in the early 1960s, was the American Sign Language, and since then similar studies have been made of many others, including British Sign Language. The studies show that most of the signs used in different countries are no more alike than the words of different spoken languages, as shown in these examples:

FATHER
(British Sign Language)

FATHER
(Hong Kong Sign Language)

FATHER
(S. African Sign Language)

TRY
(British Sign Language)

TRY
(Swedish Sign Language)

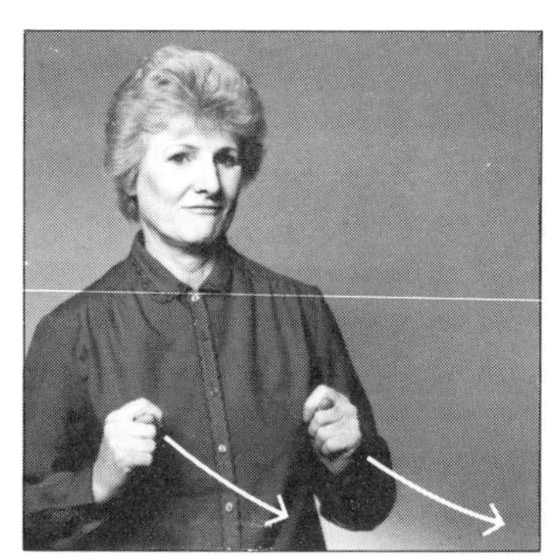

TRY
(American Sign Language)

Even the sign vocabularies of Britain and America, where the spoken language is nearly the same, are very different.

Nonetheless, since all sign languages use vision and are produced by the human body in space, different nationalities have come up with similar commonsense ways of expressing certain ideas, using imagery shared by the hearing world. For example, when we talk about time we say that the past is behind us, the present is where we are, and the future is ahead of us. Many sign languages express this idea thus:

PAST

NOW

FUTURE

This is logical. Likewise, no sign language would place the sign for eating on the elbow or describe a tall man using this sign:

SHORT

This kind of visual commonsense has produced similar language patterns in all national sign languages. As a result, signers from different countries can adapt to each others' vocabularies much more easily than speakers can, and can develop a common communication code for temporary use. However, each language remains distinct and there is no fully international language. Whatever parallels may be found in other sign languages, the grammatical features described on the following pages should be taken as relating only to British Sign Language. (See Glossary under 'Gestuno', p. 108.)

DEAF-(PEOPLE)

How do I take part in sign language communication?

First it will be useful for you to know the signs that identify whether a person can hear or is deaf. These signs refer to 'hearing' people as a group, and deaf people as a group, as well as meaning able or not able to hear.

HEARING-(PEOPLE)
(Southern version)

HEARING-(PEOPLE)
(Northern version)

1 Physical conditions

When speakers talk together, they do not need to look at each other, but they do have to be able to hear what is said. If they are too far apart or if conditions are noisy, they will have difficulty getting the message. Communication is easiest when speakers are within touching distance in quiet surroundings.

Unlike speakers, signers do not communicate best when they are closest to those watching. A signer needs space for making his own signs, and he needs to be able to see other signers from the waist upwards to get the full visual message.

So signers tend to stand or sit further apart than speakers do, and can in fact carry on conversations at distances or in situations impossible for speech. Communication may, however, be affected by poor light, or by 'visual noise' such as glare, dazzle, bold wall patterns and rapid background movements that can distract a watcher's attention.

2 Etiquette

There are good and bad manners for signers just as there are for speakers. Conventions about starting a conversation, keeping it going, taking your turn, interrupting and ending it need to be learned. Some of this behaviour is different from that used by speakers, but is right for a language based on vision.

a) Getting attention

To start communicating with a deaf person it is necessary to get his attention. If he is close enough, but looking away, this can be done by tapping his shoulder or arm. If he is further away, you can wave your hand or even an object like a newspaper. Another accepted way is to set up a vibration that will carry to the other person by banging on a convenient surface.

In a group it may be necessary to ask a bystander to relay your tap to the person you want. In a crowded room, it is quite usual for this to result in a whole chain of waves or taps until the right person is reached. With large groups (e.g. at meetings or social gatherings) the normal way to get everybody's attention is to flick the lights on and off.

Some ways of getting attention are not considered polite in the deaf community. You sometimes see children trying to turn their parent's head towards them by tugging at the chin. Adults do not accept this from each other except in close relationships, and then usually only during arguments! Waving your hand right in front of someone's face is impolite, unless you have good reason for it. The same is true of flicking the lights just to get the attention of one person in a group. Tapping a person anywhere except on the shoulder or arm is rude, and tapping too hard or too often can get you the same treatment back!

b) Showing attention

Once he has been contacted by a tap or wave, the person on the receiving end of a signed message is expected to keep his eyes

THAT'S-RIGHT

AWFUL

on the sender until a natural break occurs. The sender is free to look away from the receiver, but remains conscious of the receiver's gaze and responses. If you are the receiver, you can show you are following the messages by nodding, or you can respond, without interrupting the sender, by expressing your feelings, using signs like the two shown left.

If the sender becomes aware that the receiver has looked away he will pause or stop – so breaking eye contact is one way for the receiver to interrupt a sender.

c) Taking turns

If you, as the receiver, want to contribute to the conversation, you must first catch the sender's eye by waving. Or you can bring your hands up ready for signing. If he is prepared to give up his turn, the sender will drop his hands from the signing space. If he is just letting you in to comment, he will keep them there ready to resume as soon as you have made your point.*

* In a mixed group of hearing and deaf people, the etiquette of taking turns becomes more complicated. If hearing people use their voice to take turns from one another, deaf people will have difficulty getting into the conversation. Such behaviour is considered rude, and hearing people need to use visual ways of getting attention in these situations.

d) Interrupting

The receiver can interrupt the sender by looking away or by waving for attention. He may also catch the sender's eye by shaking his head or using a sign like this one to show disagreement.

DISAGREE

e) Finishing

The sender shows that he has finished by dropping his hands from the signing space and looking at the receiver. He may first specifically ask for a response.

What do I use for sign communication?

1 The signing space

We have already seen that the important area for sign language is the space on and in front of the body, from just below the waist to just above the head. These photographs illustrate the limits of signing space in use.

The signer uses the signing space almost as a stage on which things, people and places can be set up in relation to each other, abstract ideas can be expressed and narratives built up. A signer's hands may move anywhere within the space as he gives his message. It seems a large area on which to concentrate, but the receiver's eyes do not need to follow the movement of the hands. This is because the signer's hands give only part of the message, as will be explained below. Instead, the receiver concentrates on the signer's face and takes in the moving hands with his area vision. Only occasionally is it necessary to glance away from the signer's face to his hands. As a beginner in BSL you may need time to discover this for yourself, but until you do, you will miss the full message.

WHAT (*Type 1*)

2 The hands and arms

Movements of the hands and arms are the first things to catch the eye in BSL. These hand or *manual* signs use a variety of different handshapes and movements and are the easiest parts of BSL for a beginner to learn, though it must always be kept in mind that they do not carry the whole message.

There are three kinds of manual signs, one-handed, two-handed and mixed. A right-handed signer uses his right as the leading hand, and a left-hander his left.

a) One-handed signs

There are two types of one-handed signs:

those which are made in space (*Type 1*),

and those which touch any part of the body except the other hand (*Type 2*).

MY (*Type 2*)

Since a signer has two hands, he can sometimes make two one-handed signs at the same time (see p. 94).

b) Two-handed signs

There are three types of two-handed signs:

Type 1: both hands are moving and active whether in space or touching each other or the body.

MANY (*Type 1*)

BUTTERFLY (*Type 1*)

EXCITED (*Type 1*)

Type 2: the leading hand contacts the other, and both handshapes are the same.

Type 3: the leading hand contacts the other, but the handshapes are different.

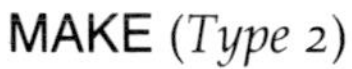

MAKE (*Type 2*)

OBJECT-TO (*Type 3*)

In some cases when the hands have made a two-handed sign, this sign can be continued with only one hand, while the other makes a new sign (see p.88) and vice versa.

c) Mixed signs

These can change from one-handed to two-handed and vice versa, as in this example:

BELIEVE

3 Dictionary form of manual signs

It is not easy to see how a sign is made when it happens in a sentence, because it is so brief and the hands quickly move on to the next one. But each hand sign has what you might call a dictionary (or *citation*) form, i.e. as it would appear in a dictionary, not as part of a sentence. Like words, these dictionary forms of the hand sign can be broken down into parts:

a) The handshape

There is a basic handshape for every sign, which may stay the same, or may change, as the sign is made. Over 50 different handshapes have been identified in BSL, some being used far more often than others. Here are three common ones.

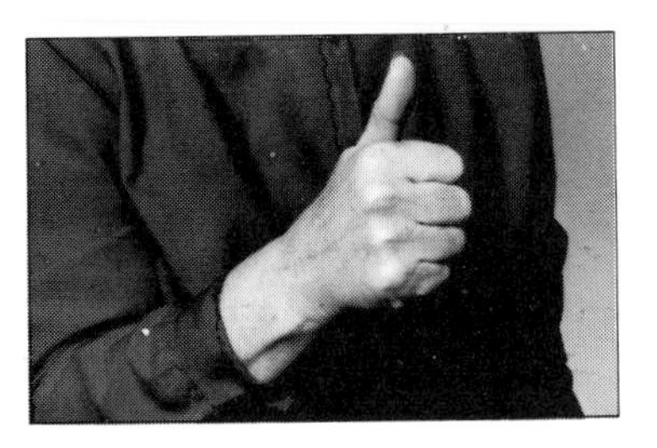

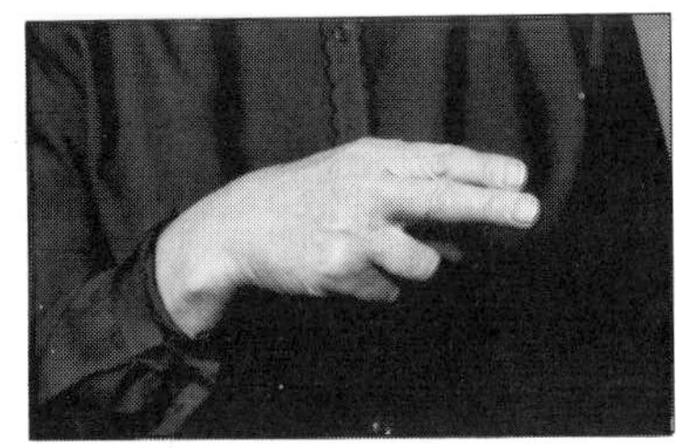

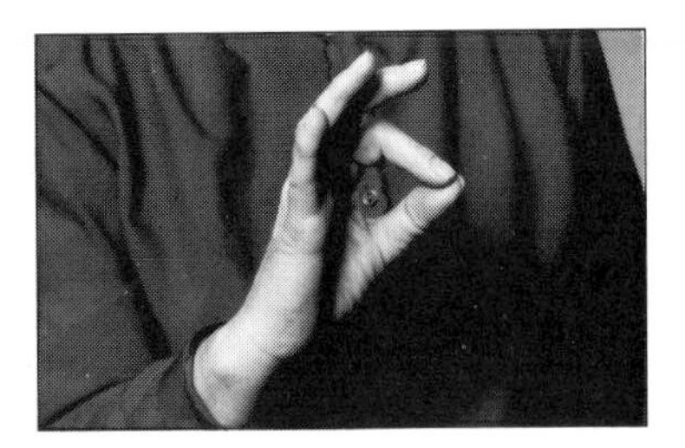

Some of these handshapes are formed from the way things are held and used, as in the following examples:

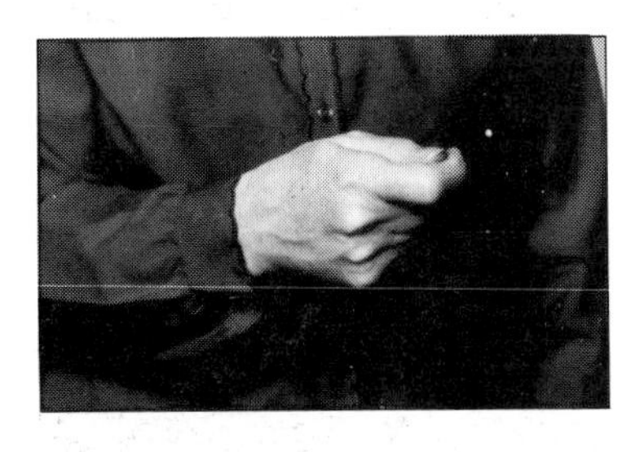

(a)

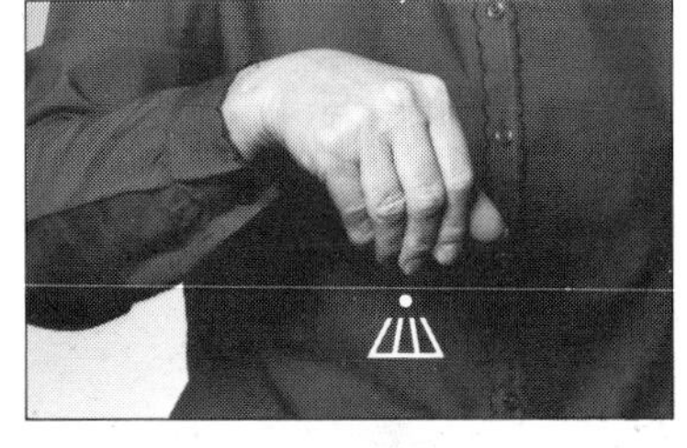

(b)

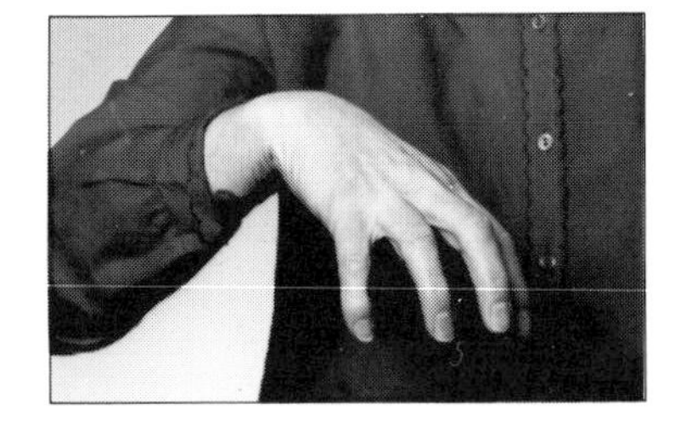

(c)

Handshape (a) comes from the way we hold certain long thin objects such as the handles of spoons, pans and so on.

Handshape (b) can suggest items that are held in, or rubbed by the finger tips, such as material, flour or seeds.

Handshape (c) is used for suggesting how we hold certain rounded objects that turn, such as door knobs, taps and jar lids.

b) *The place*

Signs can be made with one hand or two in the space in front of the body, or by touching the arms, shoulders, chest, head, parts of the face, and so on. Few signs are made below the waist and none on the right arm of a right-handed signer. In all, a signer uses about 25 different places in the signing space.

c) *The way it faces*

The direction in which the palm and fingers face in relation to the signer's body can be important. Two handshapes may be exactly the same, but the different directions can give them different and even opposite meanings.

d) *The movement*

Sign language appears to beginners to be a continuous movement, and they find it hard to see where one sign ends and another begins. This is because the signer needs to move his hands from place to place in the signing space in between making signs. But each sign has a specific movement of its own, and changes of this movement can change the meaning of the sign.

A change in any of these four parts of a sign changes its meaning, although the other three parts remain the same. The fact that each sign can be analysed in this way shows that signs are not 'random gestures', but are as precise and consistent as words in the way they are made. Look at these four pairs of signs:

A change in handshape

WRONG

TRUE

A change in place

STUPID

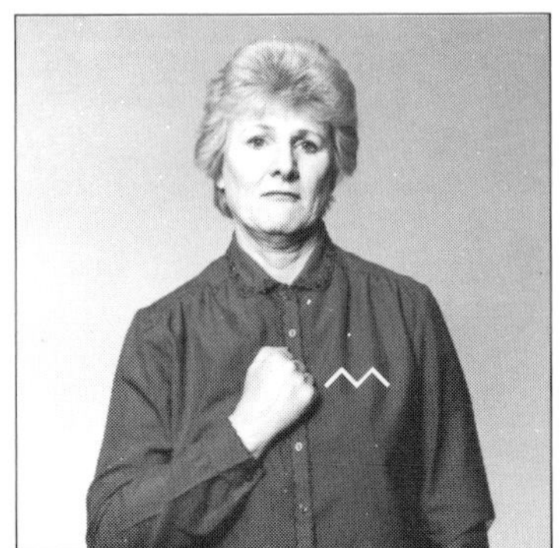

MINE

A change in palm direction

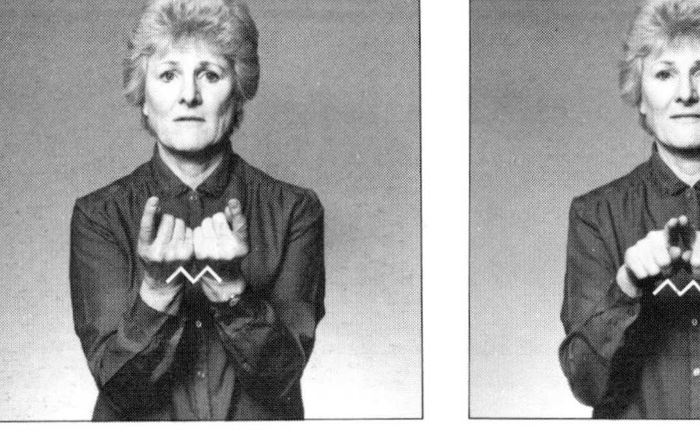

THING

SAME

A change in movement

BETTER

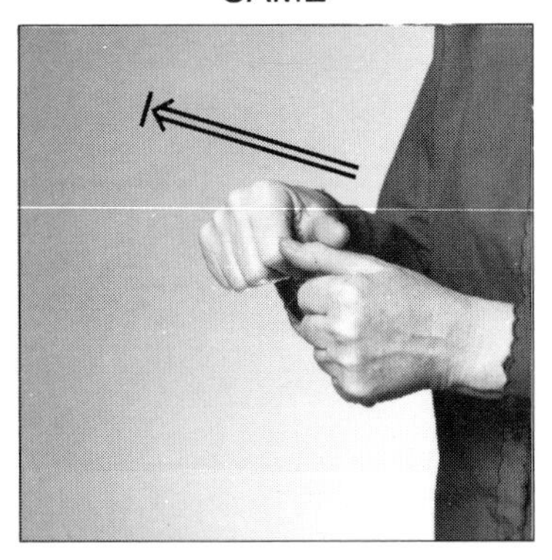

BEST

Now let us see how other parts of the body add to the message given by manual signs.

4 The face, head and upper body

Messages given by the face (both as a whole expression and through individual features), the head and body are less obvious than those given by the hands, but are just as important. This is one reason why signers concentrate their gaze on the area of the face and head. A manual sign that is supported by information from these other parts of the body is called a *multi-channel* sign, because it uses more than one means of expression to give the full message.

a) The whole face

Like a speaker, a signer uses his face to show his changing emotions. His facial expressions, however, may be heightened to perform the same functions as the tone of a speaker's voice, and this has resulted in a number of standardised expressions in BSL, such as the positive and negative faces shown here:

positive face

negative face

The face also gives important information about how an action is done, so that different expressions give different meanings to the same sign:

WATCH – suspiciously

WATCH – with surprise

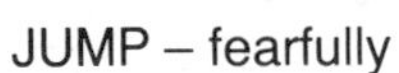

JUMP – fearfully

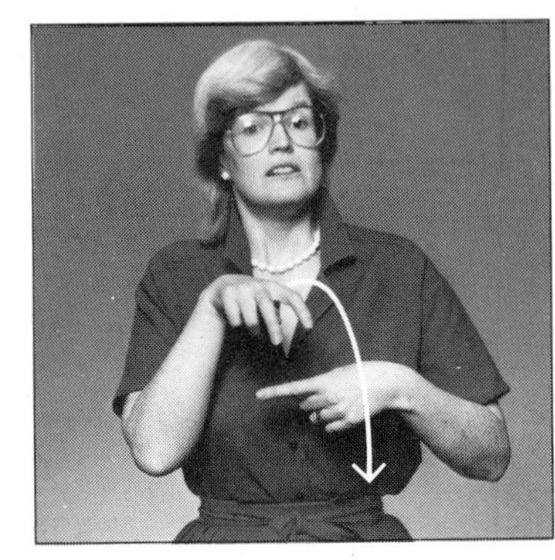

JUMP – carefully

Individual features of the face – the mouth, cheeks, eyes and eyebrows – also give meaning to a sign language message.

b) The mouth and cheeks

Movements or arrangements of the mouth and cheeks can change the meaning in several ways. They can show how an action is done:

An open mouth with the teeth clenched shows stress or effort.

A loose pout with slightly puffed cheeks suggests ease.

A loose or open mouth, sometimes with the tongue showing, implies carelessness, lack of attention or ignorance.

RUN – desperately

TRAVEL – comfortably – BY TRAIN

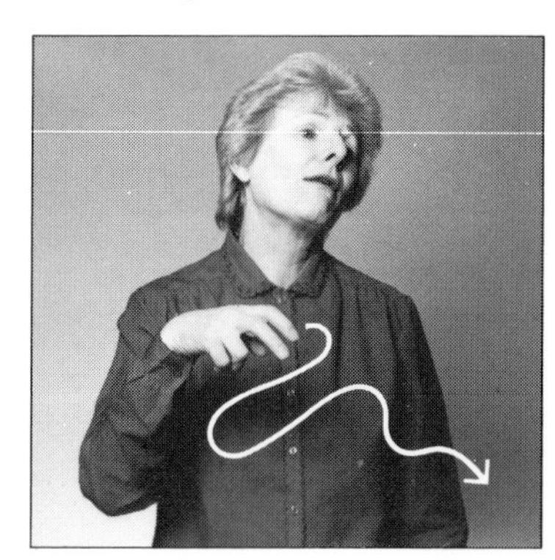

WANDER – carelessly

They can give a sense of intensity – for example, of nearness or exactness. For this the lips are pulled tight in an 'ee' shape with the teeth just showing, as in:

JUST-NOW
(near in time)
(fingertips move backward)

NEXT-TO
(near in space)

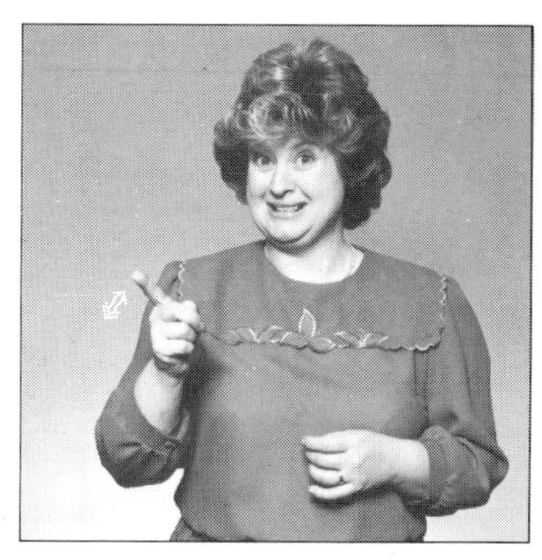

'that's the one'
(exact identification among others)

They can show variation in size and volume. For example, fully puffed cheeks added to descriptions of water, wind, rain or snow mean a heavy flow or fall. Pursed lips and sucked-in cheeks tell us that the flow or fall is light.

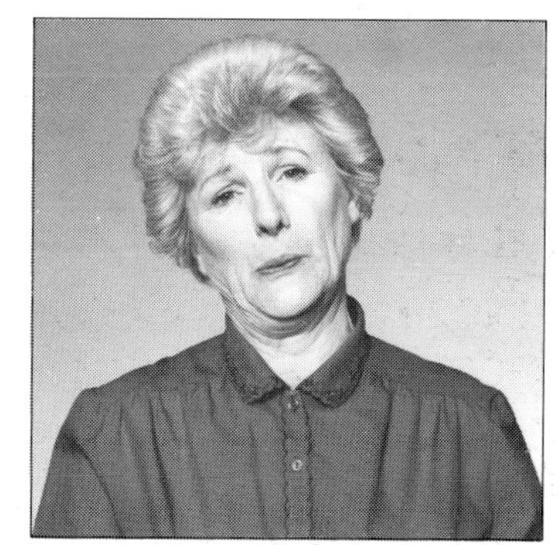

(contrasting expressions of size, volume, etc.)

This contrast is used in describing things that are large or small, fat or thin, many or few.

Other mouth and cheek patterns are made by drawing air in or blowing it out. They may have developed from physical reactions, such as the release of tension. One example is the sign sometimes translated as 'At last', where the lips may make a speech pattern like 'ba' as air is blown out.

'At last' (start)

'At last' (finish)

GOOD

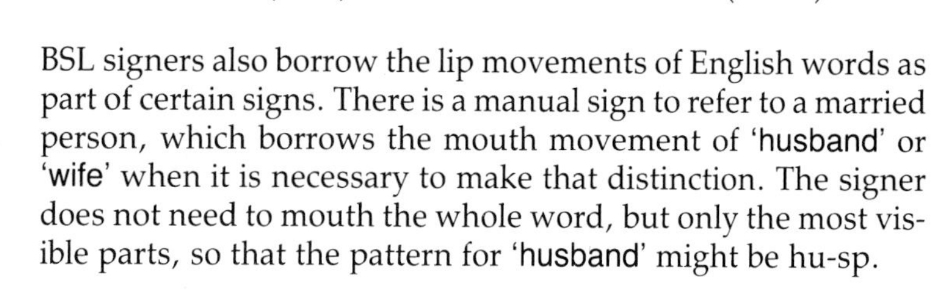

BSL signers also borrow the lip movements of English words as part of certain signs. There is a manual sign to refer to a married person, which borrows the mouth movement of 'husband' or 'wife' when it is necessary to make that distinction. The signer does not need to mouth the whole word, but only the most visible parts, so that the pattern for 'husband' might be hu-sp.

c) *The eyes*

The eyes present information in several ways. First they give the face much of its emotional tone. They widen for surprise, narrow for doubt, and so on. In addition, they reinforce the information given by the mouth and cheeks about how an action is done.

Another way they give information is by narrowing to show intensity. This makes the difference between the signs FAR and VERY-FAR, GOOD and VERY-GOOD and similar pairs.

VERY-GOOD

A third use of the eyes is called *eye gaze*, i.e. the direction in which the eyes look, and the way in which they move. By his gaze a signer can show where things are and where they move to, and also how they move. This will be discussed again under 'Placement of signs' on p. 91.

d) The eyebrows

Movement of the brows cannot really be separated from what the eyes are doing. They knit when the eyes narrow and rise when the eyes widen. But sometimes they seem to take the lead, particularly for questions.

Raised eyebrows, with head tilted forward and eyes widened go with questions expecting the answer 'Yes' or 'No'.

'Are (you) coming?'

'Is that enough?'

Knitted eyebrows, with eyes slightly narrowed and the body sometimes tilted back usually go with WH-questions. When?, Where?, Who?, How?, etc.

'Which one?'

'Who's that?'

These last two photographs also show examples of simultaneity in BSL, which is described on p. 94.

e) The head

The head is particularly important in punctuation. It can break up sentences with brief nods and tilts. Head movement is also important, along with eye gaze, in placement (see pp. 89–91).

Like speakers, signers in Britain use nods and headshakes to mean 'yes' and 'no', but a signer's use is more systematic. A nod makes a positive statement, a headshake a negative one, so that with one manual sign two opposite meanings can be given.

HUNGRY (nod)
'I'm hungry'

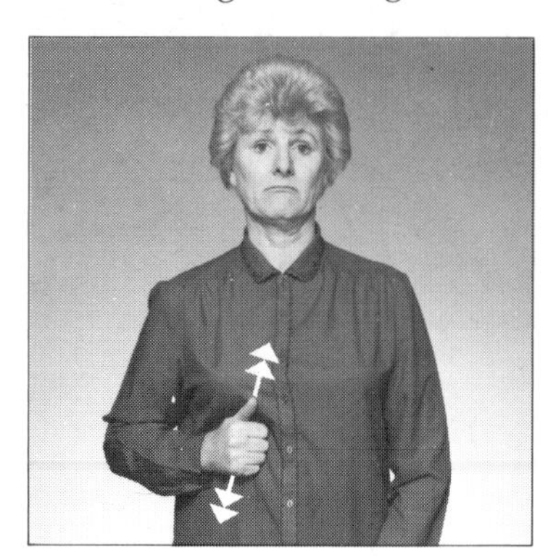

HUNGRY (headshake)
'I'm not hungry'

f) The body

The body means the whole trunk from the waist up. BSL uses the body's natural behaviour as part of its sign message. Anger or shock may make the body tense, so tension is part of the signs related to these feelings. Look at these other examples:

A forward tilt shows astonishment, interest, curiosity.
A backward tilt shows defiance, suspicion.

'Let's see'
(body tilts forward)

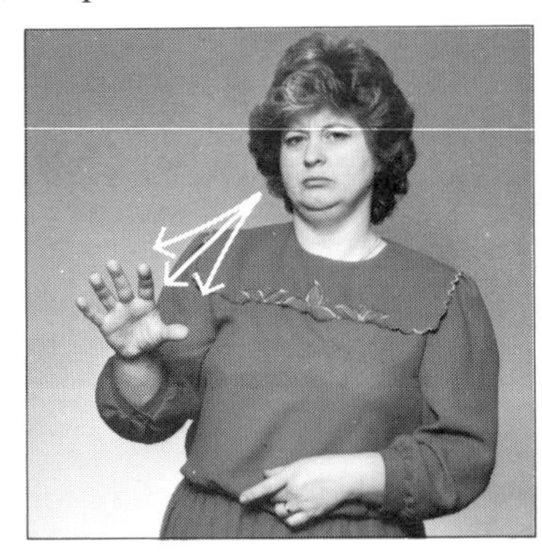

WON'T
(body tilts back)

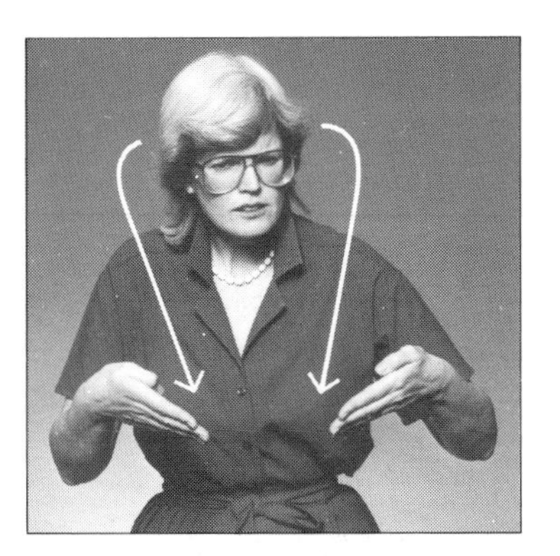

CONCENTRATE
Hunching implies effort.

PROUD
(with rising chest)

DISCOURAGED
(with falling chest)

The body also uses changes in tension to give information about how an action is performed, to show intensity and to add emphasis. Shifts in the body's direction and mime-like movements (such as the movement of the shoulders in walking) are important in reporting events (see p. 90).

To sum up, to understand BSL you need to be able to read the messages given by all the different parts of the body involved. Let's now look more closely at what happens on the hands, but keep in mind that they tell only part of the story.

What the hands can tell us

1 The sign – picture or symbol?

Speakers use words to give things a name, and signers use signs. But what are signs? Are they like pictures in the air, 'imitative and transparent in meaning', or are they symbols just as words are? The short answer is that if signs were just pictorial (or *iconic*) no-one would need to learn sign language – its messages could be understood without difficulty.

However, there is a grain of correct observation in the former description. Some signs do present a visual idea of their meaning, some have a passing resemblance, and others look nothing like it. The same relationship of form and meaning is found in other visual communications, such as painting and sculpture.

This statue is instantly recognisable as a man on a horse. Not only that, it is recognisable as a particular man, King Charles I of England, and gives us a clear picture of his features.

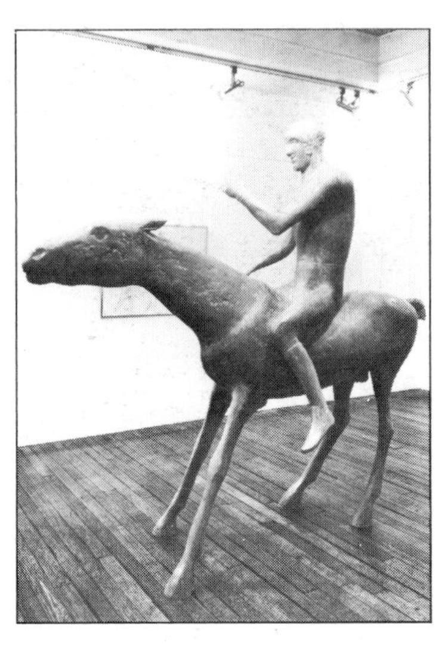

This statue by Elisabeth Frink is also a horse and rider, but it is not identifiably a particular person. It is less a picture, more of a symbol.

This Seated Figure by Henry Moore derives from the human form in a way which is almost entirely symbolic. It is like a code to which the title is the key.

In sequence these form a kind of visual spectrum:

King Charles statue	Elisabeth Frink statue	Henry Moore statue
more pictorial	←——————————→	more encoded

This also occurs in BSL. Some signs are called *transparent*. Beginners can guess them without too much trouble. The sign for DRINK is an example.

Other signs are called *translucent*. These are not so quickly recognised. The one for CHEAP suggests something is being reduced. When you know its meaning, the link between form and meaning becomes clear.

The third group of signs is completely encoded and gives no visual clue. An example is WHY. So, in BSL, the spectrum runs:

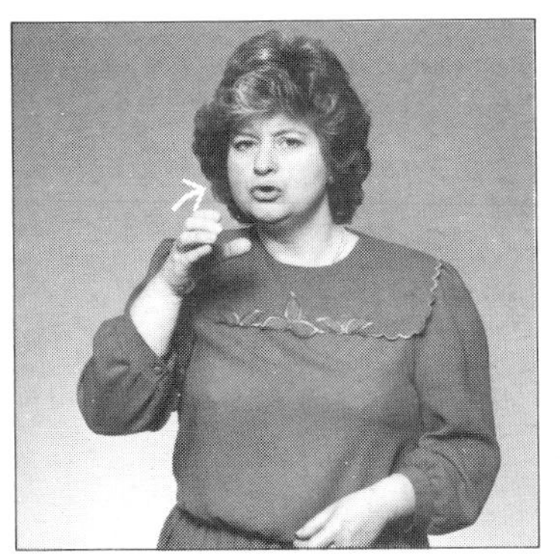

DRINK

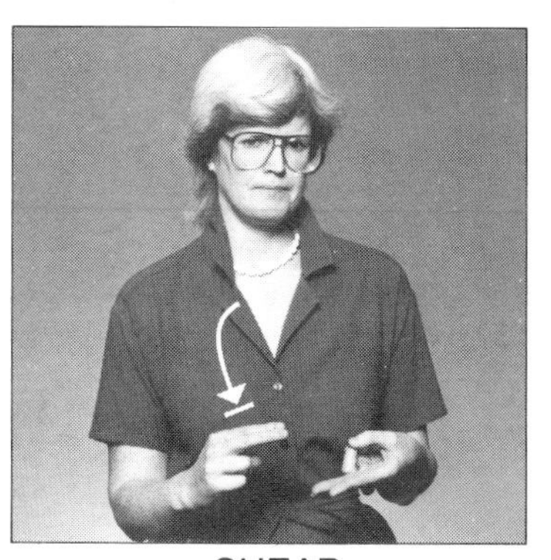

CHEAP

WHY

More pictorial ⟵⟶ More encoded

For adult beginners it may be easier to recognise pictorial signs, but learning these signs first can raise the false expectation that all signs are as easy to recognise. This can lead to confusion, because even transparent signs become less pictorial when they come off the dictionary page and onto the hands. In the long run it is better to concentrate on how a sign is used, rather than why it is made the way it is. Nevertheless, as you learn, you may find it helpful to refer to the following description of how some groups of signs are produced.

2 Iconic signs

Signs with an iconic or pictorial origin can be made in three ways:

i) The fingers or the whole hand outlines the object's shape:

The outline may be the same size as the real thing or it may be bigger or smaller.

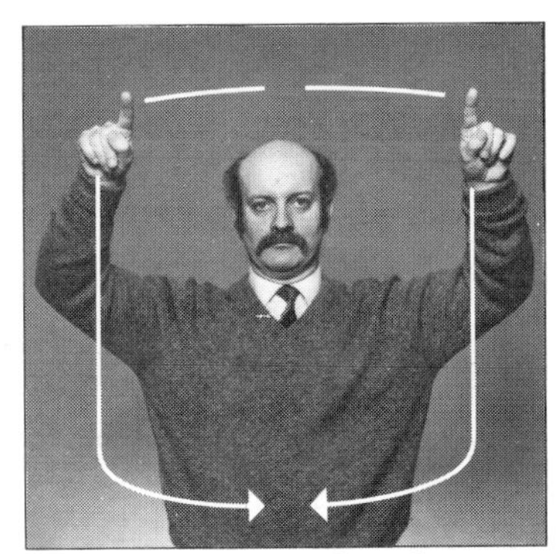

large rectangular object
e.g. poster

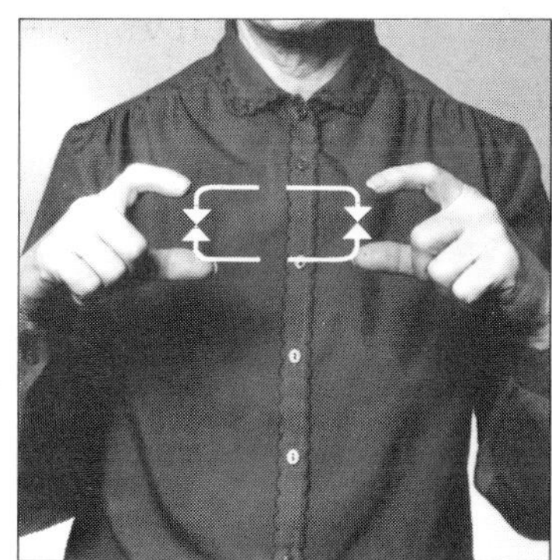

small rectangular object
e.g. business card

narrow defined area
e.g. PATH

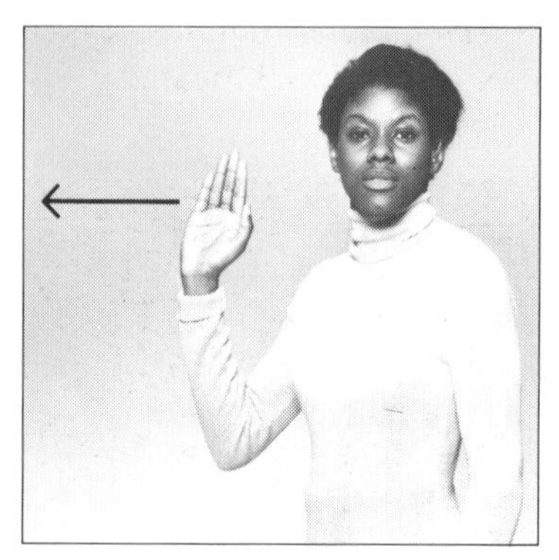

upright surface
e.g. WALL

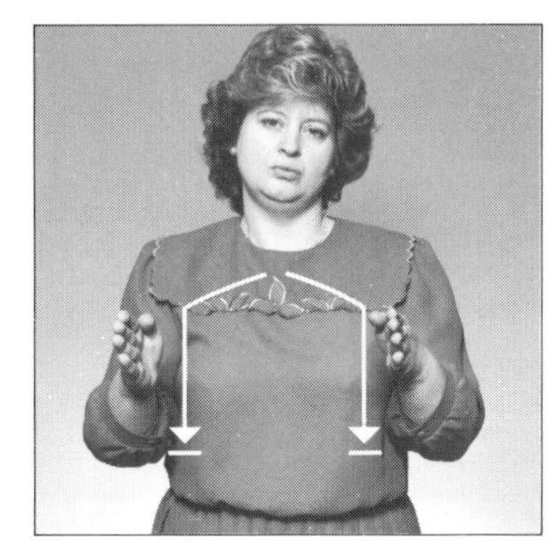

flat-sided object
e.g. HOUSE

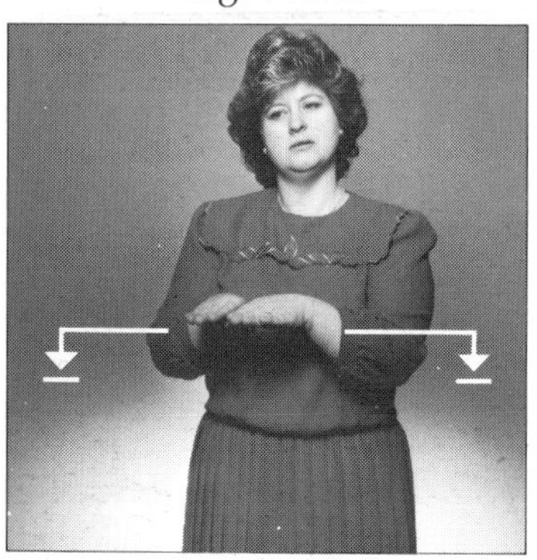

horizontal surface
e.g. TABLE

flat round object
e.g. table mat

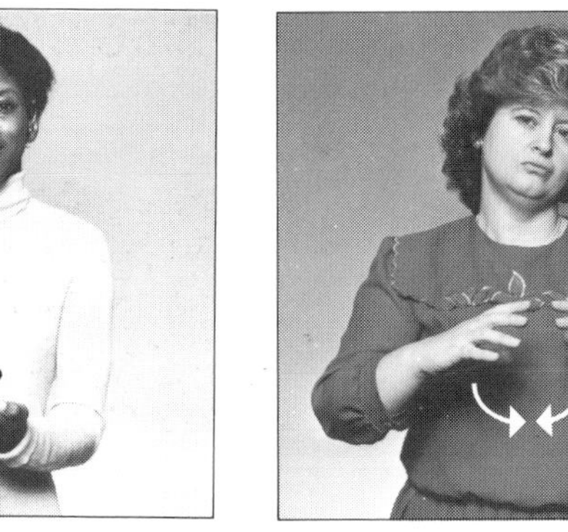

curved object
e.g. melon

tubular object
e.g. a length of pipe

ii) The signer imitates grasping and handling an object, often giving additional meanings by changing the movement.

MUG

'Drink from a mug'

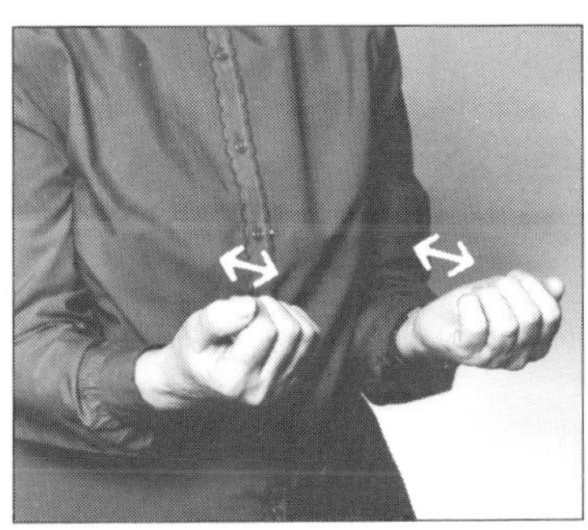

DRAWER

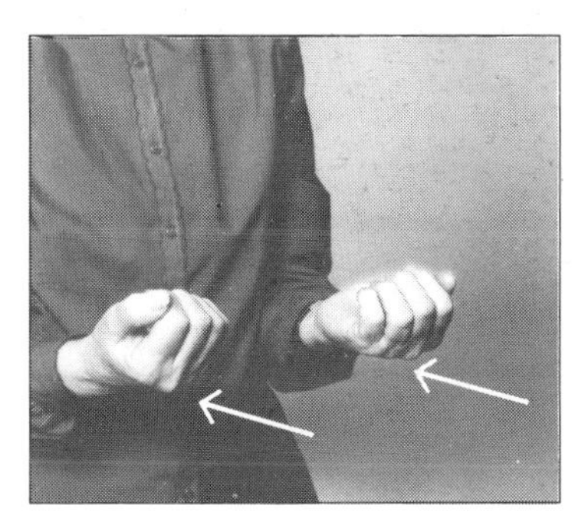

'Open a drawer'

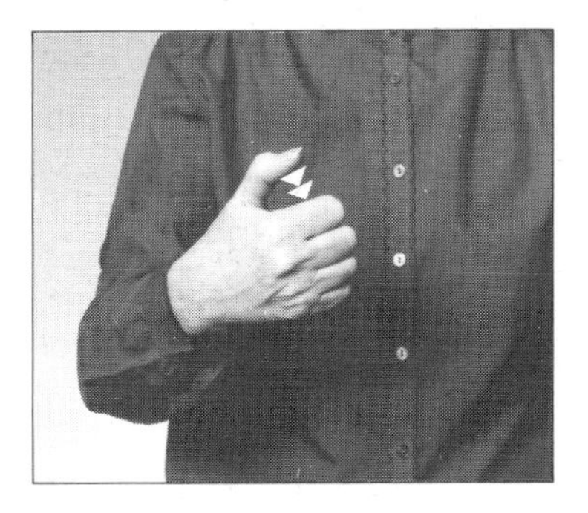

LIGHTER

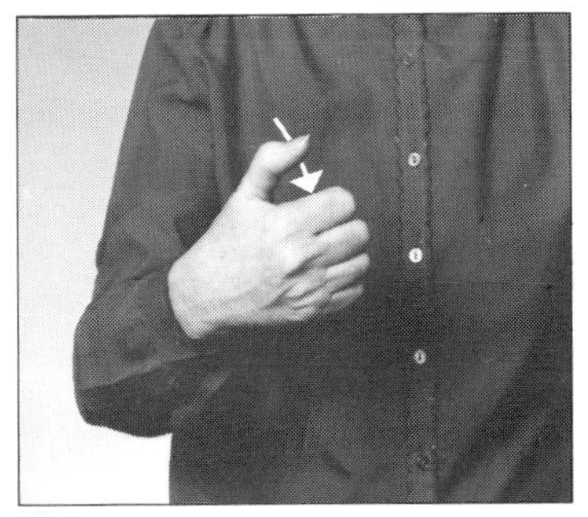

'Operate a lighter'

CIGARETTE

'Smoke a cigarette'

CAR

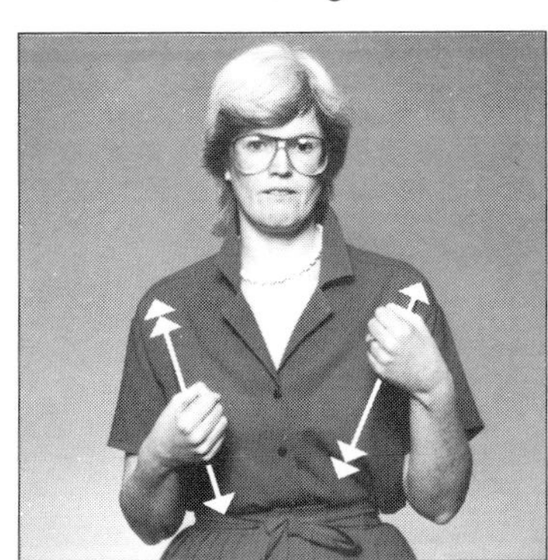
(able to) DRIVE

iii) The hand itself is the object, or part of the object. It can act as the object, giving an extra meaning:

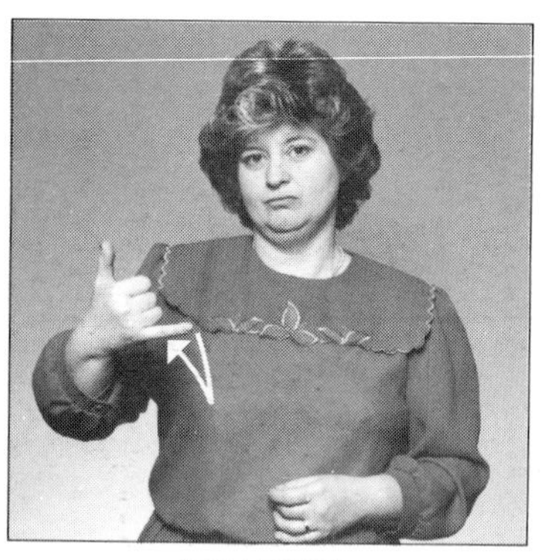
TEAPOT

'Pour from a teapot'

SCISSORS CUT

DOOR 'Open a door'

The sign for mixer shown in the photograph below means a kitchen mixer or blender. The same or similar handshapes with movements of different size and speed can be used to show various kinds of rotating action (see overleaf).

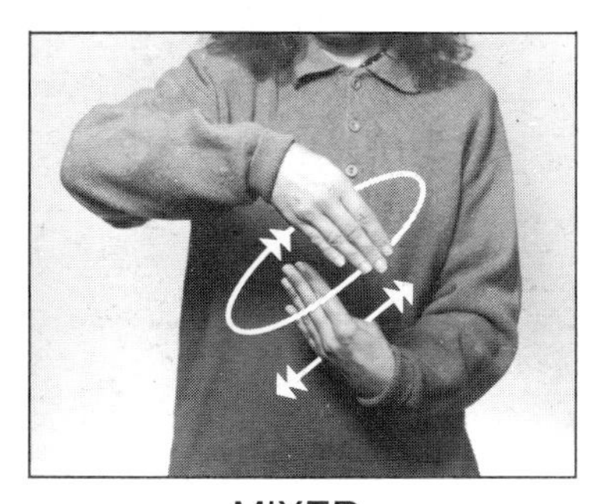

MIXER

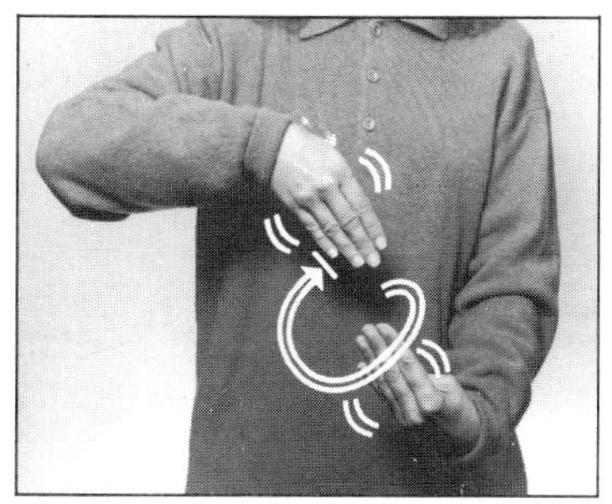

'Mix in a mixer'

HAND-MIXING
(right hand moves)

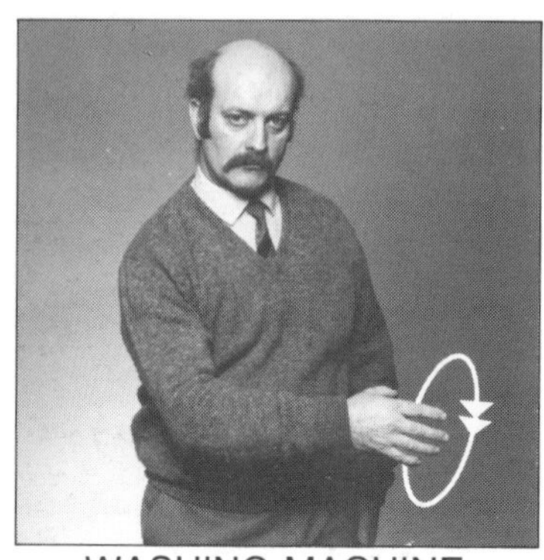

WASHING-MACHINE

CEMENT-MIXER

These three ways of creating signs are so versatile that they contribute heavily to the vocabulary of BSL. Many of the handshapes used are known as *classifiers*, which are described further below, using examples from group iii.

Classifiers

You have just seen (above) that certain handshapes and movements can be used to represent a teapot, a door and scissors. The teapot handshape can only be moved in a few ways, so the meanings it can give are limited. But some handshapes can be moved in ways that give a whole class or group of different meanings. These handshapes are called *classifiers*.

The following handshape often represents a person's legs. It is used in the signs STAND, JUMP, KNEEL, WALK, TRIP, FALL, GO-UPSTAIRS, DRIBBLE-A-FOOTBALL, DIVE, RIDE etc.

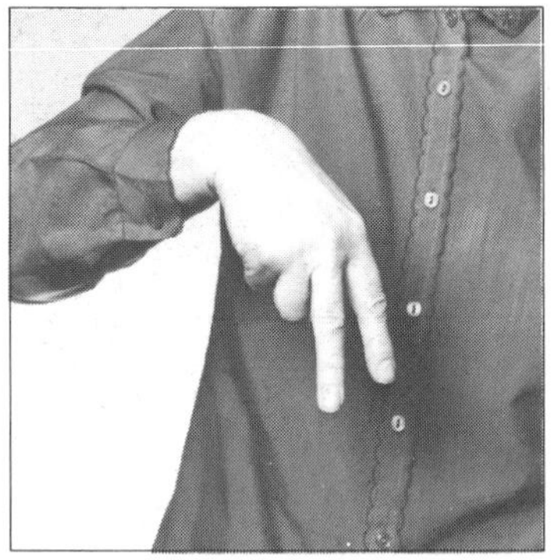

'Legs' classifier

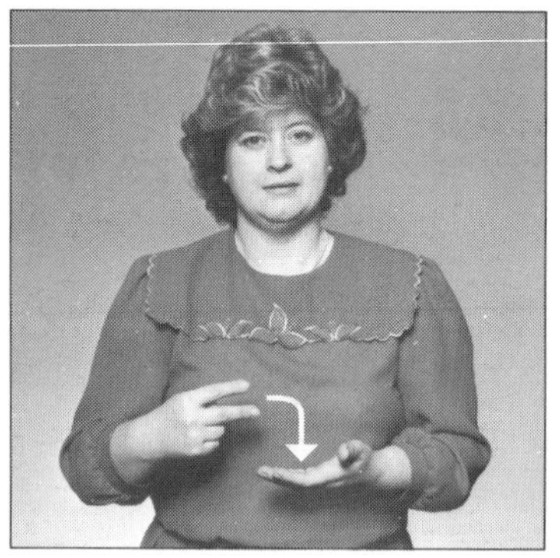

STAND-UP

But the same handshape in a different place, with a different direction represents a person's eyes and is at the root of signs LOOK-(AT/UP/AROUND), STARE, READ, SIGHT-SEEING and so on.

EYES

LOOK-UP

This open-handed sign (left) represents a beam of light and means the light is on. The closed-hand sign means the light is off. Opening and closing the hand turns the light on and off.

Depending on where it is placed, the light can be a table lamp, a standard lamp, a ceiling light, a spotlight, even the sun itself. Opening and closing the hand flickers or flashes the light, keeping it open makes a steady beam. These handshapes are the root of the signs for TRAFFIC-LIGHTS, ILLUMINATIONS, SUNBATHE, SEARCHLIGHT, HEADLIGHTS, and so on.

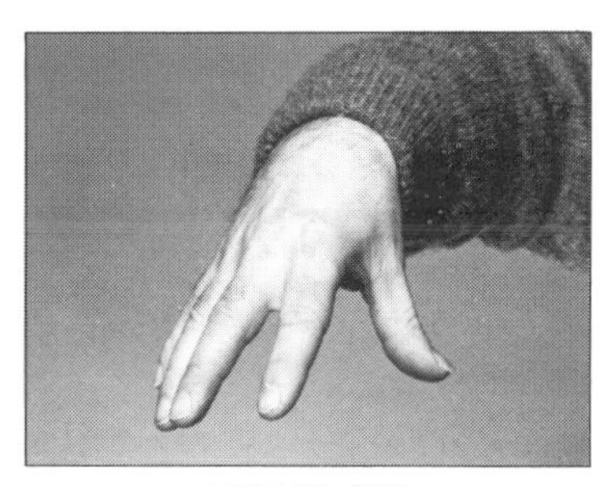

LIGHT-ON

LIGHT-OFF

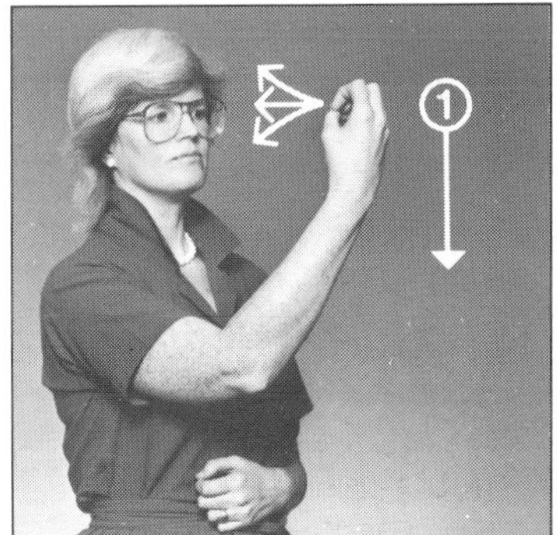

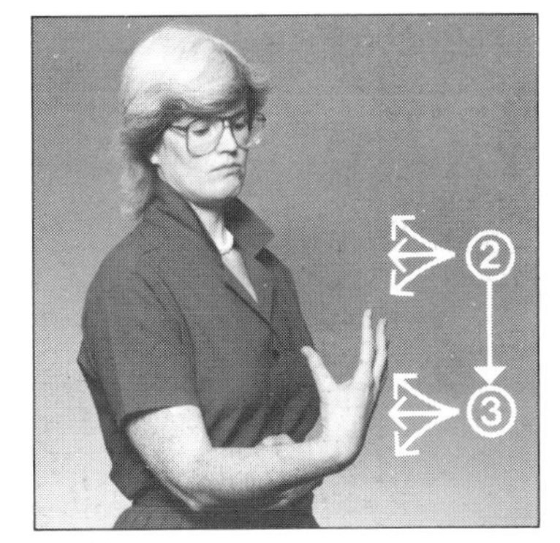

TRAFFIC-LIGHTS

There is another form of classifier which is used to take the place of a sign that is not easy to move about – it is called a *proform*. Take the case of the sign for 'car' shown on p. 70.

CAR is a two-handed sign. The signer grasps and turns a steering wheel, and would have to move himself about to show the movement of the car – a cumbersome business. So after making the sign CAR he uses the proform shown below.

This flat hand is easy to move forwards and backwards, up and down and sideways in different ways. But it does not easily go around tight corners. (The wrist cannot bend far enough.)

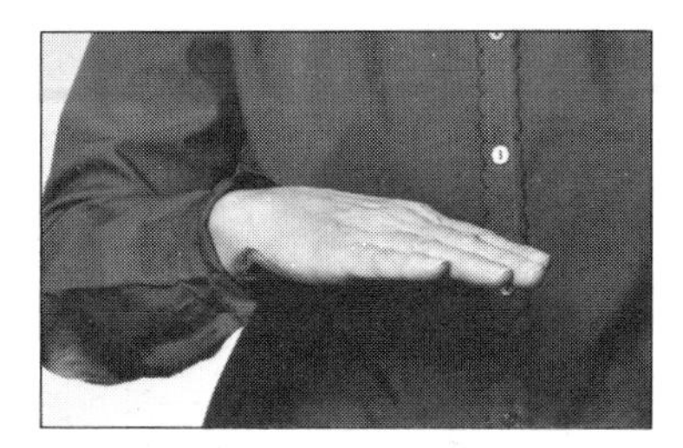

Flat hand proform

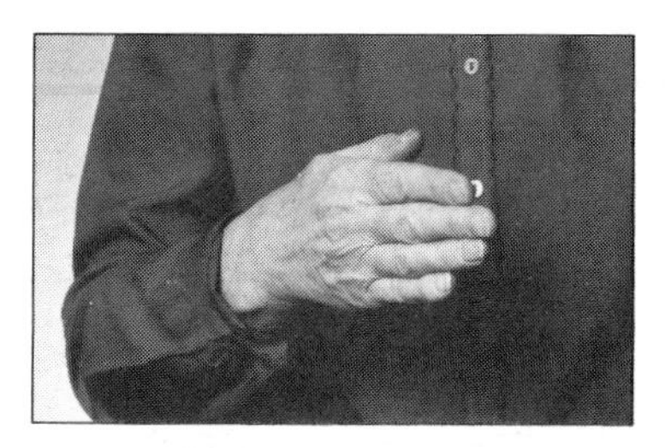

Upright hand proform

So, the signer's car sometimes turns corners with this upright hand (above), which is easier to bend. In this upright position the hand can also be the proform for a parked car, or for a parked or moving motor cycle or bigger vehicles like a coach, depending on which sign has gone before.

The flat hand can also represent a number of things that are flat, or nearly so – the foot, a book, a box, a bed, a table, a mirror, a picture, a window and so on. You can put all these things on surfaces such as floors, walls and shelves, which are also represented by this handshape, moved a short distance (see p. 68).

The next handshape shows a person. It can be placed and moved in various ways to give different meanings. For example, it can be used to show which way a person is facing. In the first photo he is facing away from you, and in the next example, towards you. The person can be shown to move quickly, slowly, to wander or move directly, and so on.

'person facing me'

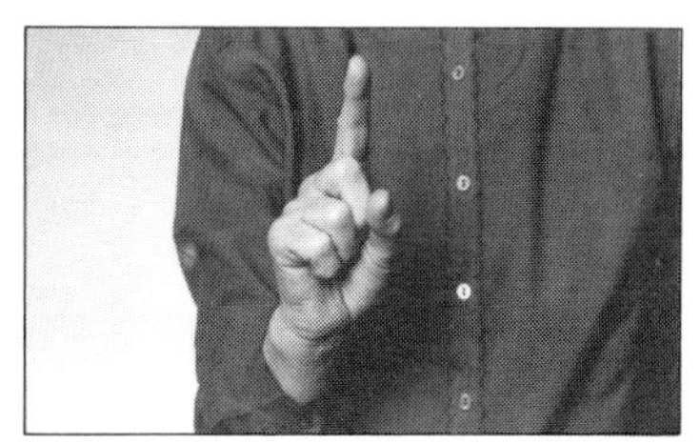

'person facing you'

When two hands are used, two people are involved. We can show them side by side, or one behind the other; they can meet, pass each other, change places, and so on.

'side by side'

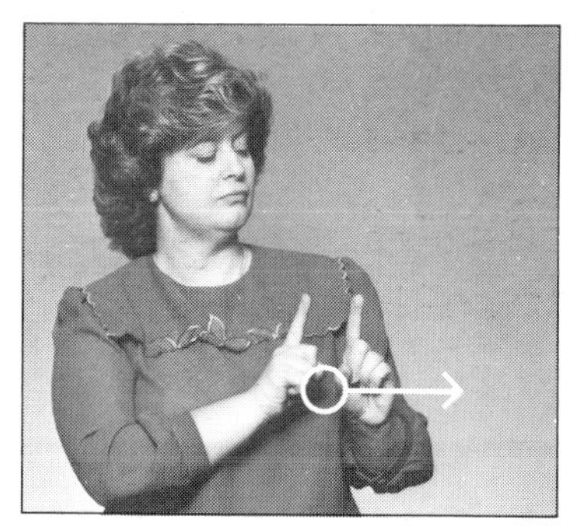

'one behind the other'

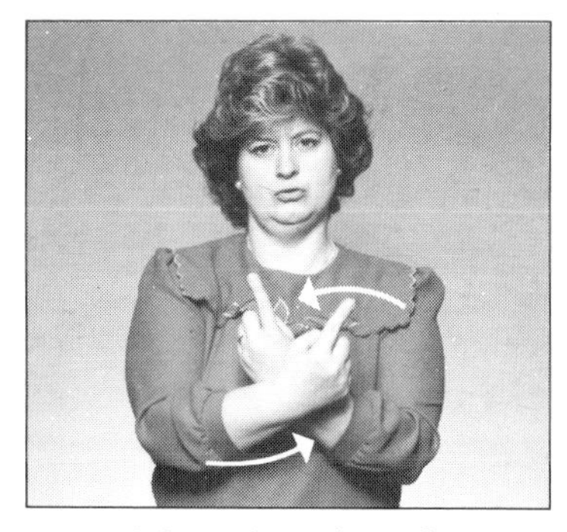

'changing places'

To represent a line of people (more than four) this handshape is used on both hands. With different movements we can show a circle, a single file, or rows of people, and whether they form a straight or ragged line.

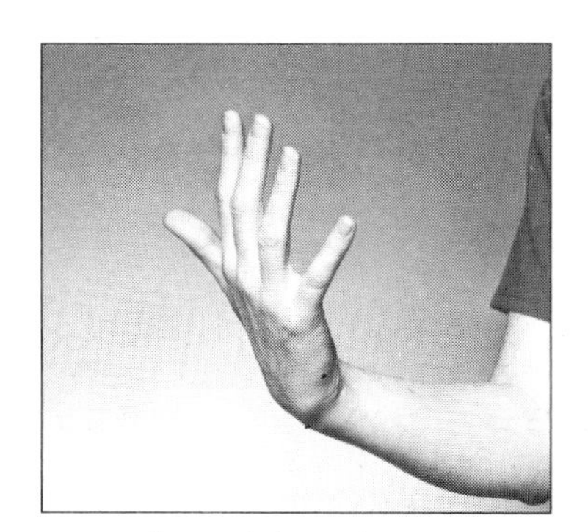

'people' proform

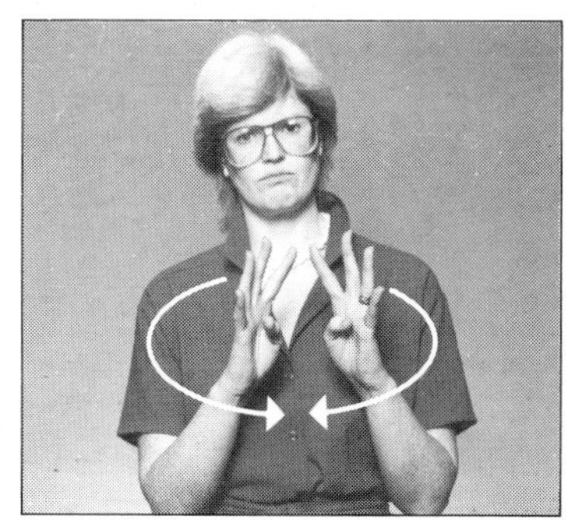

'neat circle'

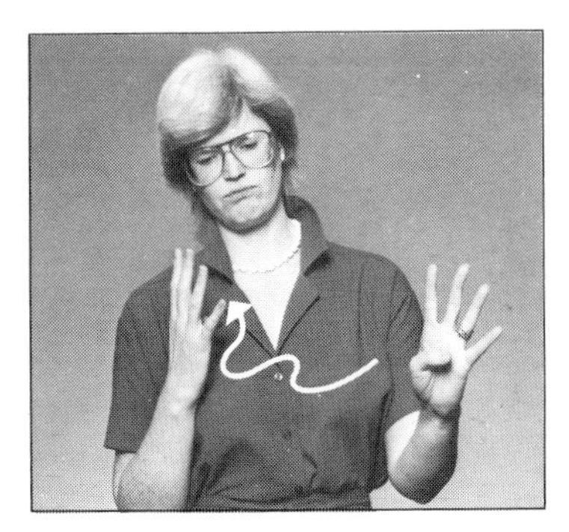

'straggling queue'

To indicate large numbers of people, whether marching in columns, milling in crowds, or seated, this palms-down handshape is used. Again, the hands can be moved to show how people are moving or sitting.

'jostling crowd'

'spectators in tiers'

Other handshapes which stand in for signs as proforms are:

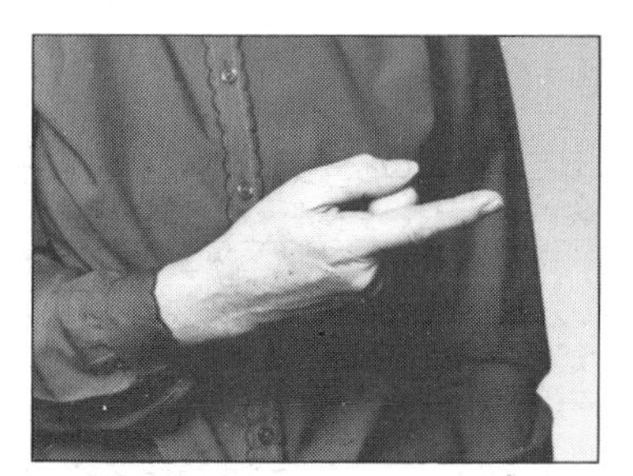

Short, thin, tubular objects, e.g. cigarettes

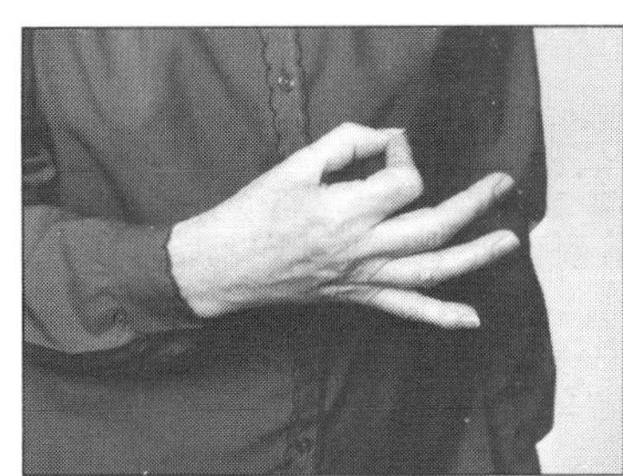

Small, thin, circular objects, e.g. button

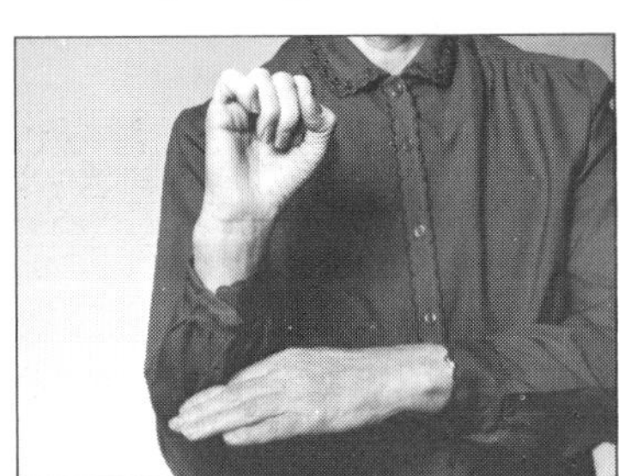

Person or animal's head

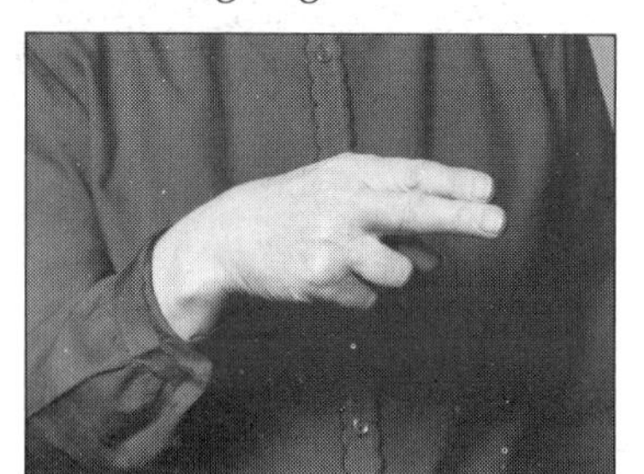

Longer thin objects, e.g. knife

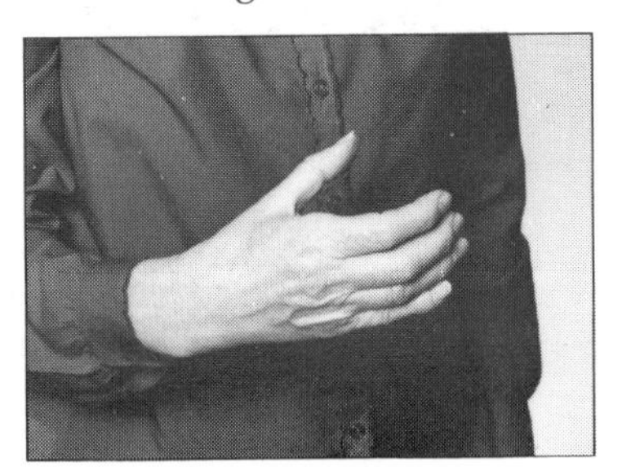

Large, round objects, e.g. bottle

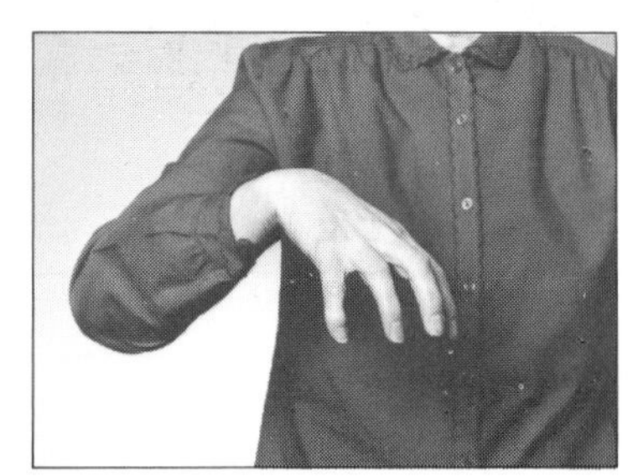

A mass, e.g. a big house

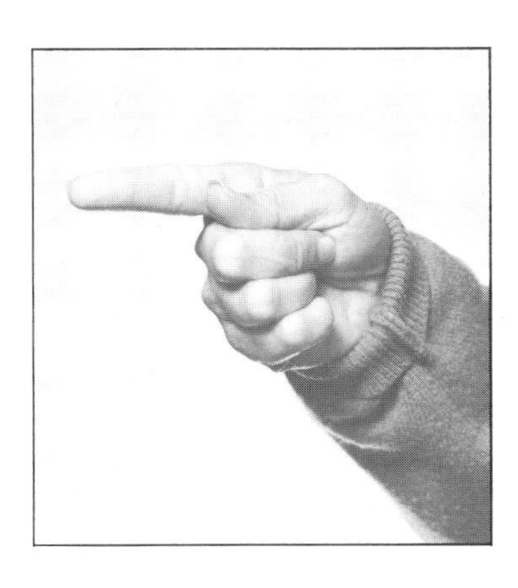

3 Other groups of signs

Many of the basic signs in the BSL vocabulary, whether or not they give an obvious visual meaning, can be fitted into convenient groups for reference purposes. Some of these groups are described in the following section.

a) Pointing

The natural gesture of pointing is used to give these meanings: ME, YOU, YOU-TWO, ALL-OF-YOU, HE, SHE, IT, THEY, THIS, THAT, UP, DOWN, HERE, THERE and so on, depending on direction and movement. The sign THAT'S-THE-ONE (p. 61) also developed from this gesture. Pointing is also important in Placement, and is referred to again on p. 89.

b) Possessives

Signs like MINE and YOUR are made with a clenched fist as if holding something. This first handshape is moved in different directions, according to where people are or have been 'placed' for reference, to show ownership. A sweeping movement makes the sign plural, as in THEIR.

MY

HIS

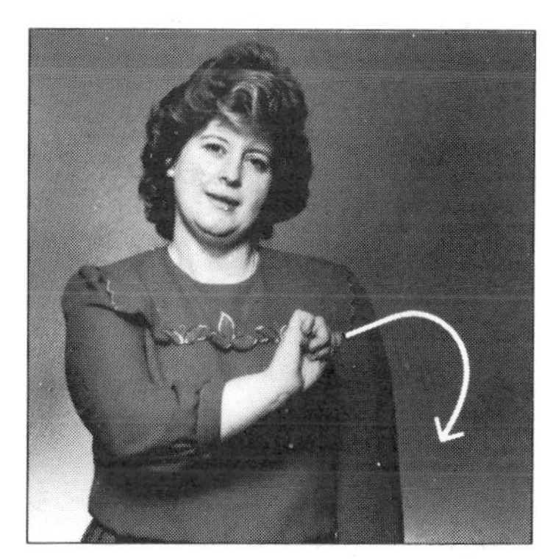

THEIR

Note that either hand can be used to sign HIS. Although a right-handed person normally favours his right hand for signing, he will use the other when it is more convenient.

c) 'Thumbs up' and its opposite

The BSL sign meaning 'good' is the same as the British 'thumbs-up' gesture. In different places, with different movements it gives meanings including RIGHT, CORRECT, AGREE, CLEVER, NICE, as well as BETTER and BEST (see p. 58). It is also a common greeting sign in the deaf community. If the thumb represents 'good', its opposite, the raised little finger, is the symbol for 'bad' (see *Negatives* below). Like 'good', this handshape has given rise to many different meanings, according to how it is placed and moved. These meanings include WRONG (p. 57), ILL, FAIL, POOR (quality), QUARREL, FIGHT, WORSE, and so on.

d) Negatives

You have seen (p. 64) that BSL can say 'no' or 'not' with a shake of the head and with or without a negative face (p. 59). Another way of giving the negative meaning of a sign is to change the way it is made, by twisting your wrist at the end of the sign, so that the palm faces upwards. This movement sometimes becomes a sign in its own right, meaning things like 'didn't', 'haven't' or 'not there' according to the context.

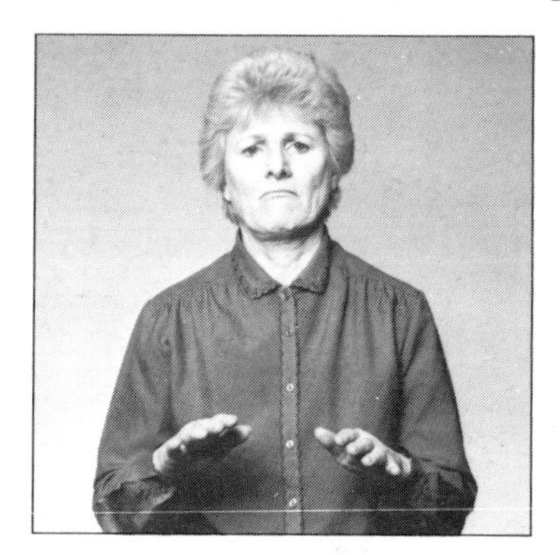

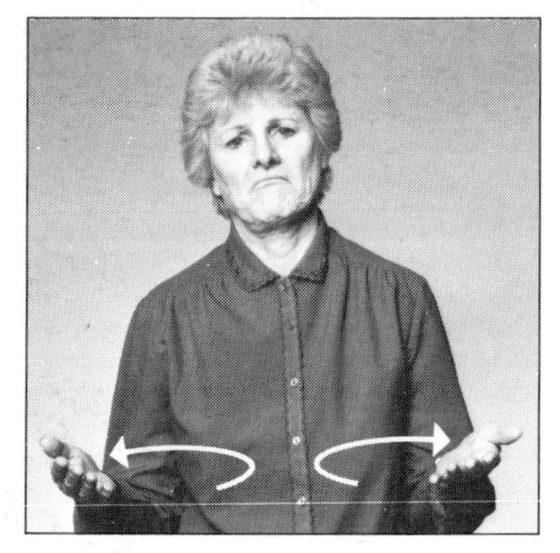

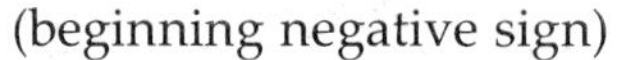

(beginning negative sign) (ending negative sign)

Two-handed signs make this movement with both hands and one-handed signs with the hand in use. Signs you can negate by this twisting movement include WANT (DON'T-WANT), SEE (DIDN'T-SEE), GOOD (NO-GOOD, USELESS), BAD (NOT-BAD), WHY (WHY-NOT?), WELL (NOT-WELL) and AGREE (DISAGREE). In each case, the original sign is changed either in handshape or position (or both) as this example shows and is held for a much shorter time than normal before these twisting movements.

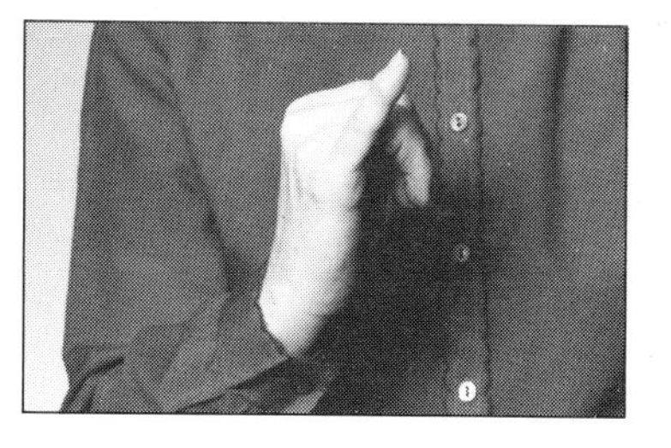

BAD

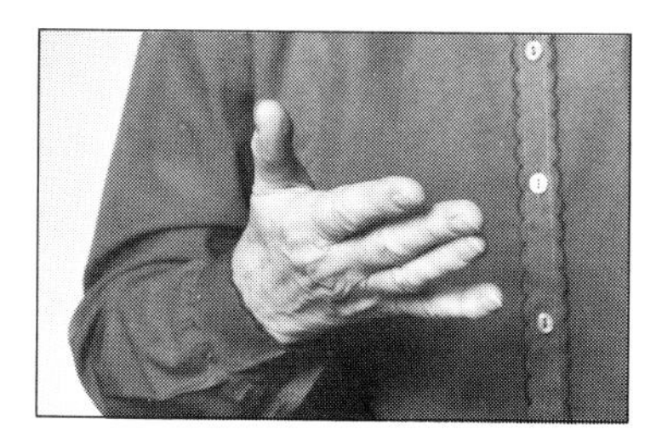

NOT-BAD

NOTHING

With a different kind of negative movement you can make the signs for DON'T-LIKE, DON'T-BELIEVE, DON'T-KNOW and WON'T. There are other specifically negative signs that you will learn as you go along, for example, NOTHING.

All of these signs are made with a negative facial expression and may also include a headshake.

e) *Numbers*

The signs for numbers may have arisen from the natural human tendency to count on the fingers, but they go much further. In BSL there are several number systems used in different areas (see p. 80). The one shown here is used mostly in the south of England.

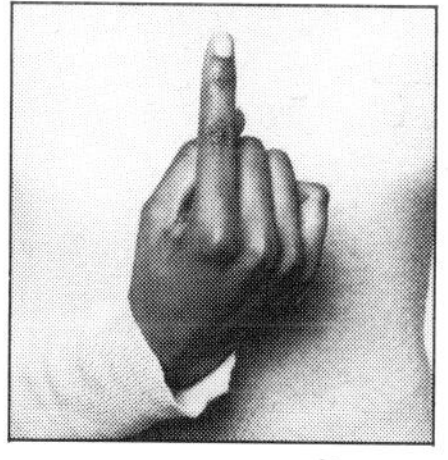

ONE

TWO

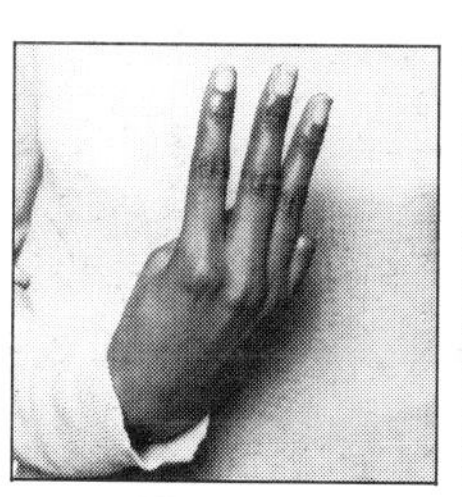

THREE

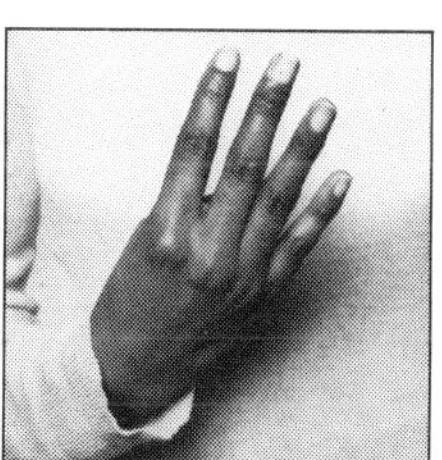

FOUR

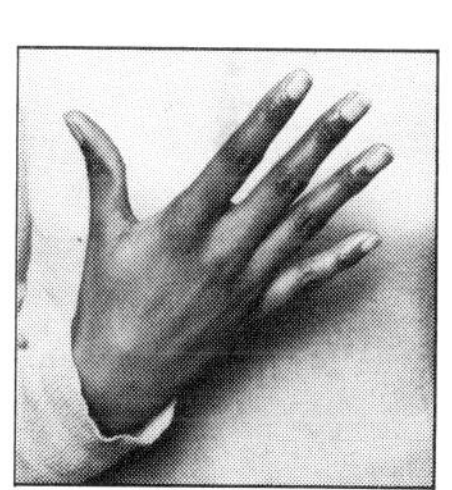

FIVE

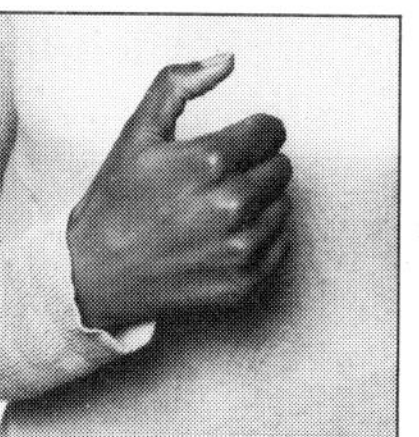

SIX

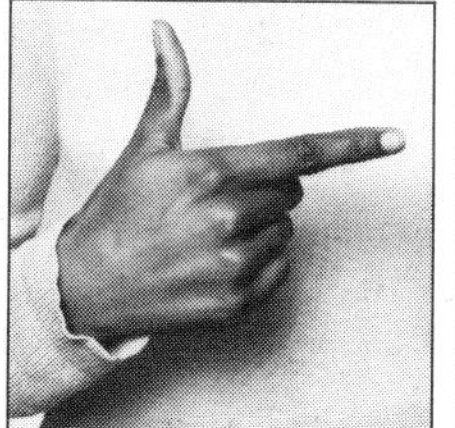

SEVEN

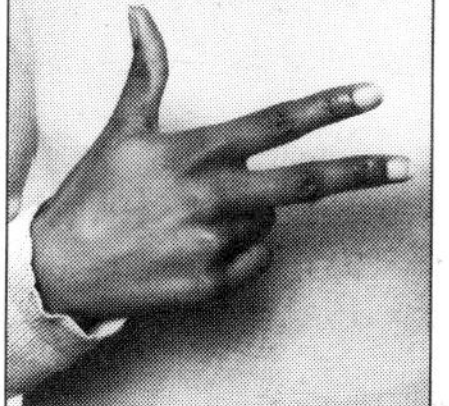

EIGHT

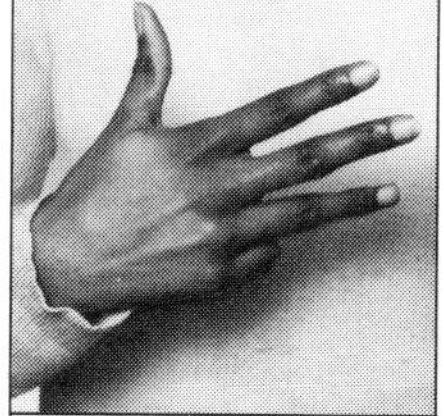

NINE

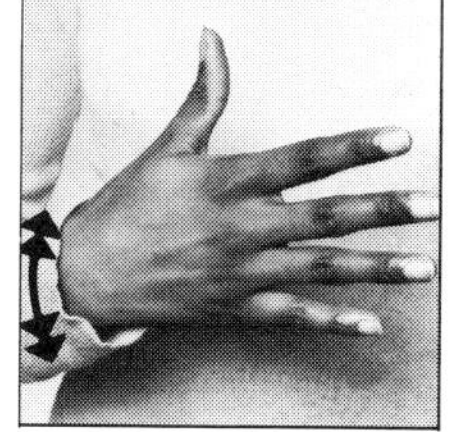

TEN

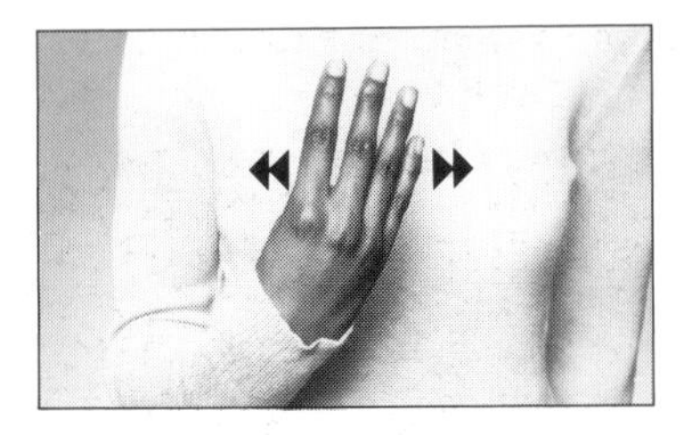

FOURTEEN

In this system, for two-figure numbers beyond 20, the hand moves slightly to the right after making the first number, changing to the second number as it moves. For three-figure numbers, e.g. 152, the first two may be made in the same place, then the hand moves forward or right for the third. This arrangement can also be seen in the other systems unless prevented by the way individual signs are made. Compare the SIX shown on page 79 with that used in northeast England and in the Manchester area.

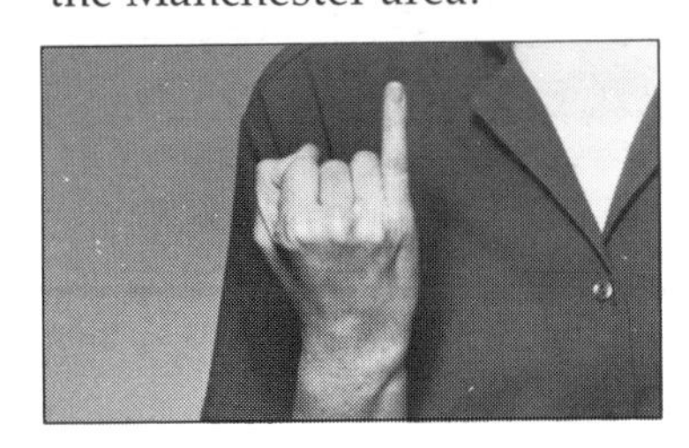

SIX
(northeast England)

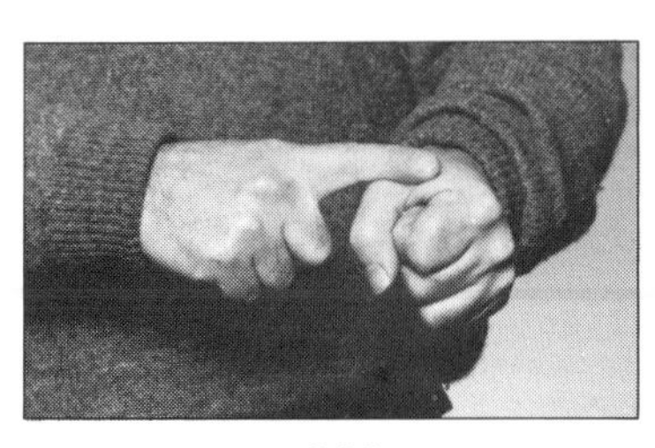

SIX
(Manchester)

With separate signs meaning 'hundred', 'thousand' and 'million', a signer can produce any number he needs with any of these systems.

In telling the time, these numbers are made in the ordinary way for phrases like 'twenty past eight', 'half-past three', 'a quarter to twelve' (see p. 103). This sign for 'half-past' is accepted in most regions, as are these two signs for 'quarter', based on the old and new fingerspelled Q.

HALF-PAST

QUARTER
(modern Q)

QUARTER
(old Q)

In each system there is a special movement to show the hour, e.g. two o'clock. Two examples are given here:

TWO-O'CLOCK
(southern England)

TWO-O'CLOCK
(northeast England)

In the southern system, a similar movement is used to show first, second, third, and so on.

When a number sign starts near the mouth, it shows pounds sterling. When it moves outward from the nose, it indicates age.

THREE-POUNDS

FOUR-YEARS-OLD

The following sign, with its wiggling movement, can be translated as 'how many?' or 'what number?'. If the same handshape and movement is made on the nose it means 'how old', and on the cheek it is WHEN. The hands moving in this way thus indicate an unknown number (of things, people, years, days, and so on). (See also the sign MANY on p. 54.)

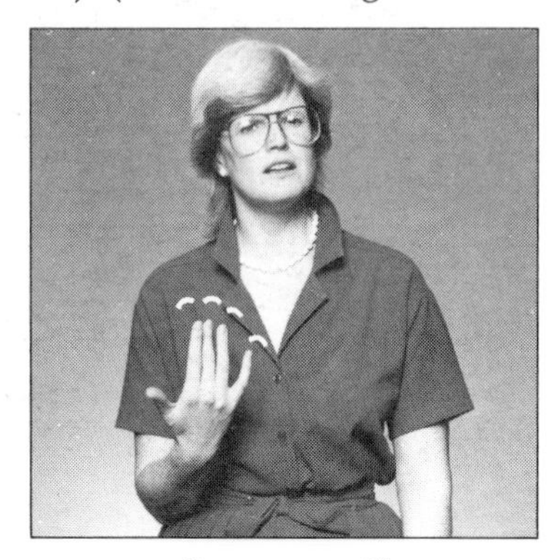

'how many?'

There are other ways of incorporating numbers into signs, particularly in association with time. This is discussed on p. 100.

4 Borrowings from English

Languages always borrow from each other when they are in frequent contact. English has borrowed from French, German, Latin, Greek and others. Since the users of BSL live in an English-speaking country, and receive their schooling in English, they have naturally made similar borrowings.

a) Mouthing

In the section on the use of the face, it was explained that the signs HUSBAND and WIFE used a mouth movement to show the difference. There are other signs that use English mouth patterns in this way, and some signers use mouthing continually while signing BSL.

b) Fingerspelling

The hands can be shaped in ways that represent the 26 letters of the English alphabet (opposite), which can then be used to spell out English words, or to make new signs. However, you should not place too much emphasis on learning this alphabet as an ABC. Though English words are sometimes spelled out in full, fingerspelling is only a minor feature of BSL and is best learned as it arises.

The modern two-handed alphabet

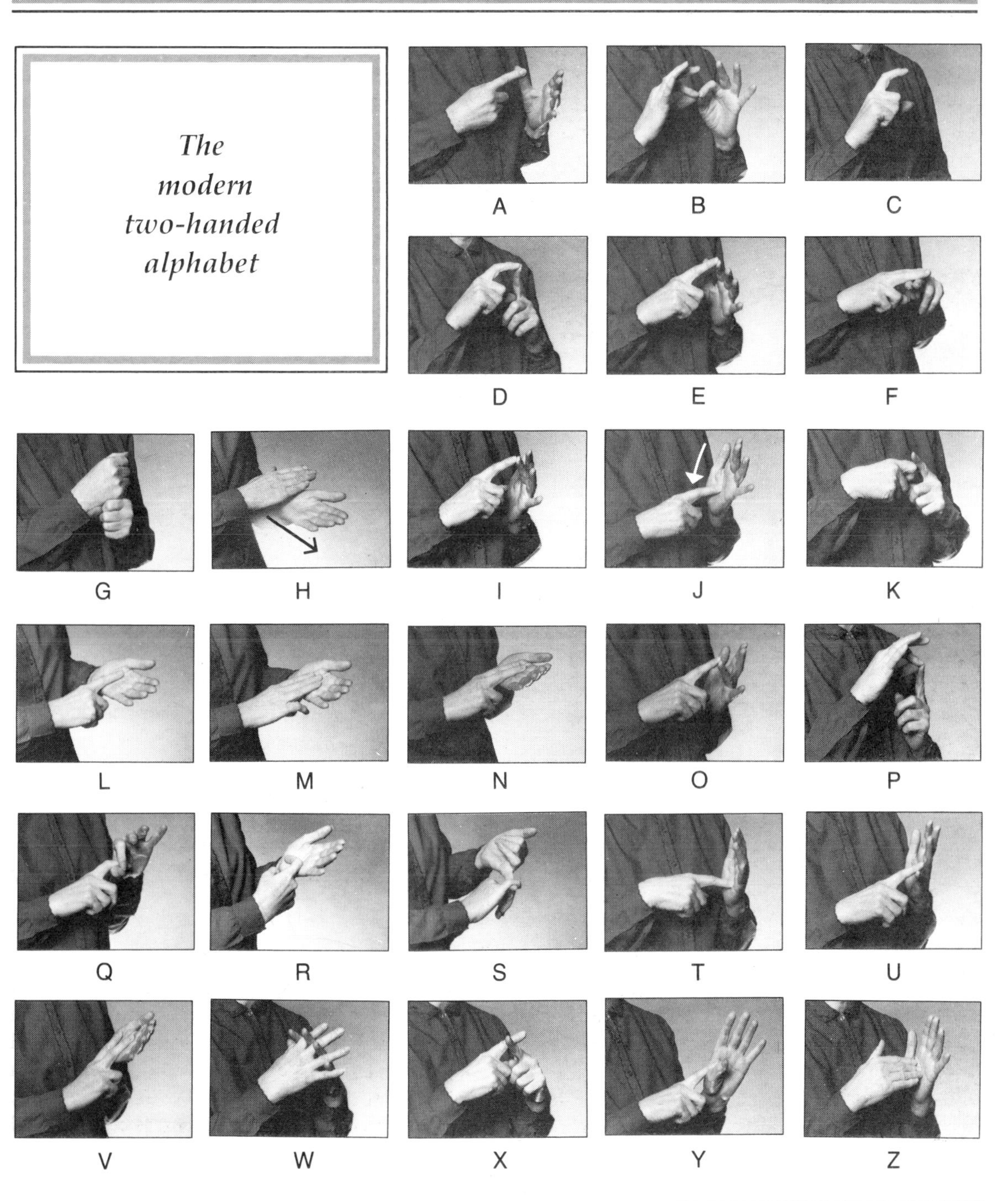

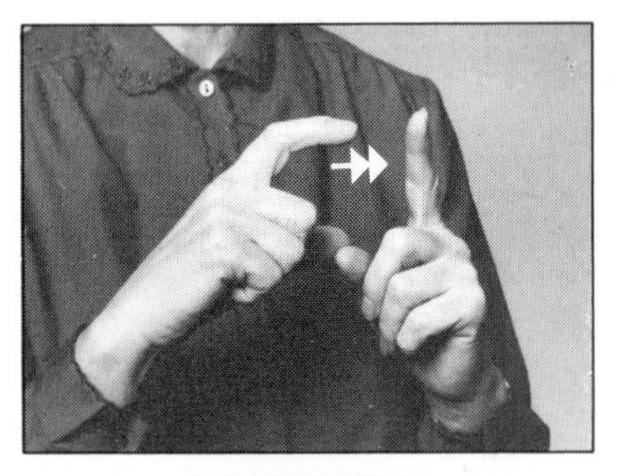
DAUGHTER

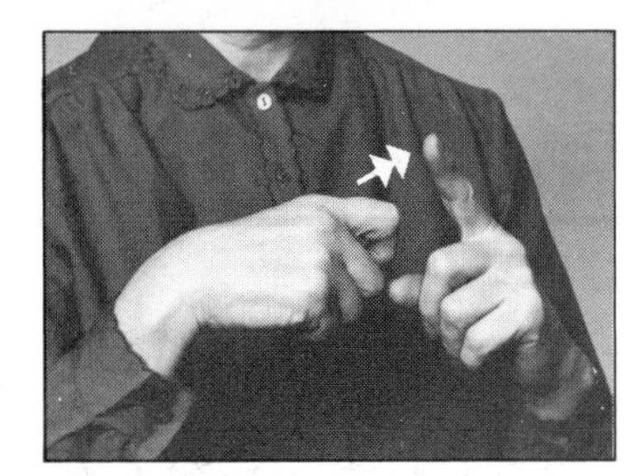
KITCHEN

A number of signs are made by a repetition of the fingerspelled initial letter of an English word. FATHER, DAUGHTER, BIBLE, KITCHEN and GOVERNMENT are some examples.

Days of the week from Monday to Friday are also signed by using initial letters (except in Scotland where there is a different system). The months are signed by spelling shorter names out in full, again with a special pattern. Only the first three or four letters of longer names are used, e.g. F-E-B, S-E-P-T.

The initials of organisations (e.g. BDA, BBC) take on a sign pattern. Some of the shorter English words 'out', 'but', 'if' can be fingerspelled very rapidly to make a sign. The most important example of these is the verb 'do'.

Some personal or place name signs come from the initials of the English name, such as G-B for 'Great Britain', or the full name is spelled out if it is short, e.g. B-O-B.

Place names often use fingerspelling patterns, in which a few letters represent the whole name, and are made rapidly with special movements and handshapes. For example, 'Bristol' can be signed B-L, 'Newcastle' N-C, 'Birmingham' B-H-M. Other place names may use the initial letter only for all or part of the sign, together with a mouth pattern.

c) *Signs Supporting English*

Some deaf people reverse the direction of the loan. If English is their first or preferred language, they may borrow from BSL to make English more visible. This results in what has been called 'Signs Supporting English' (or sometimes 'Signed English') which was the basis for the 'combined method' (see p. 107). The latter has now returned to favour in several British schools.

TREE

5 Borrowings from other sign languages

Improved communication among deaf people of different countries has led to some borrowing from each others' sign languages. In Britain, the sign for 'tree' used to be made by outlining the trunk, branches or foliage. In recent years, this American sign (left) has become popular.

The World Federation of the Deaf (see p. 112) has also encouraged its member countries to use nationality signs preferred by the countries concerned. As a result, some of the following foreign signs have become increasingly familiar in Britain.

JAPAN
(make a triangle)

NORWAY

DENMARK

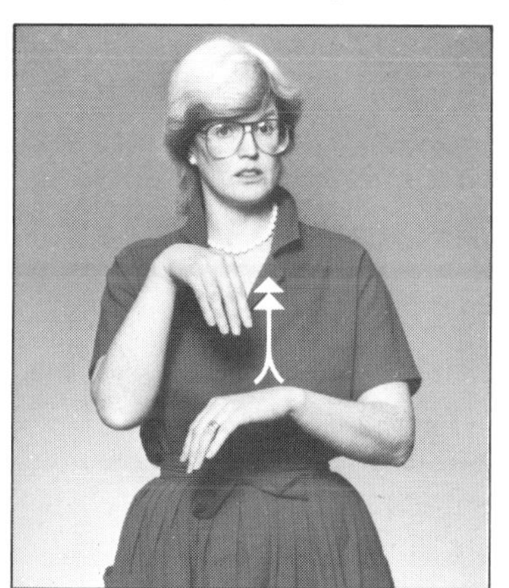
SWEDEN

FINLAND

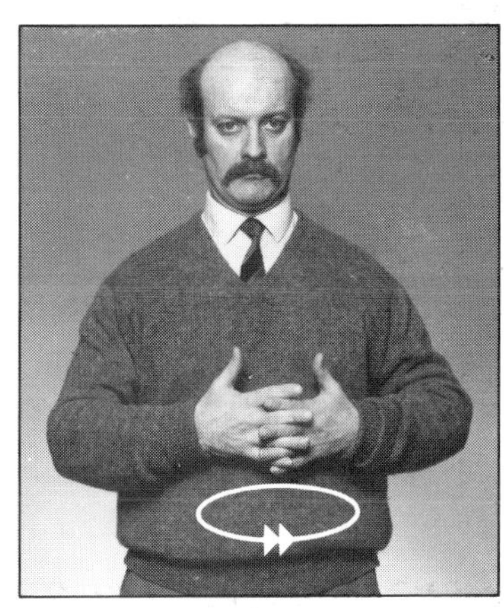
USA

6 Name signs

In sign language, visual names are more useful than spoken ones. BSL has several ways of creating visual name signs for people and places. They include:

a) The use of fingerspelled initials or complete words (see pp. 82–84).
b) The depiction of a characteristic of appearance or behaviour.
c) The use of a sign related to all or part of the English name.

Both people and places can be named according to some characteristic of appearance or behaviour. These BSL signs were created a long time ago to describe the characteristics of certain countries at that time, but are still used today:

FRANCE
(twirled moustache)

GERMANY
(1914 helmet)

RUSSIA
(Communist salute)

Personal name signs may not be so long-lasting. Children may give each other names, but change them as they grow up to suit changing situations, unless the person concerned is satisfied with her childhood name. A sign language teacher may give her students name signs for convenience, based on something they are wearing, their hairstyles, and so on at the time of the first meeting, and these name signs will last for the duration of the course. But in permanent relationships this type of name sign will be based on a more lasting characteristic of the individual concerned.

'wears ear-rings'
(convenience name sign)

'non-stop signer'
(long-term name sign)

Names that are related to English words for which there are already signs include surnames such as West, Green or Stone. A name like Washington may use the sign WASH as a cue, with a lip pattern for the rest of the word. Similarly, first names like Gloria and Angela may use the cue signs GLORY and ANGEL.

There are many signs that do not fit into any group. You will learn them as you go along. Knowing how they are made can help you produce individual signs, but you will need to use them in communication. So now we will look at ways in which complete signs are strung together with others in BSL.

How do I link things together?

1 In space

Because it is a language produced in space, BSL can make use of this space in its grammatical structure. It does this by the way it places manual signs in relation to each other, by the direction in which signs are moved, and by the type and frequency of movement. Information from other parts of the body is added to the hand actions.

a) Placement of signs

In describing the signing space (p. 53) I said that it could be thought of as a stage where the signer could set up scene after scene as he tells his story. This metaphor is closest to the truth when talking about placement. It is possible to place certain signs in the signing space so as to establish a direct relationship between them.

As a simple example, the two-handed signs SHELF and BALL may each become one-handed and be made at the same time to show that 'the ball is under the shelf'.

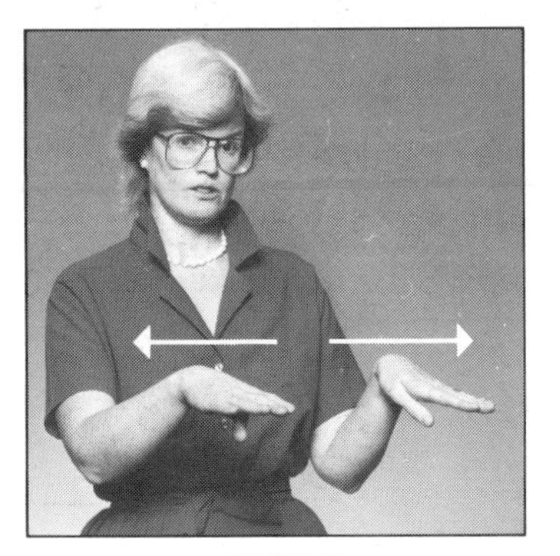

SHELF

SMALL-BALL

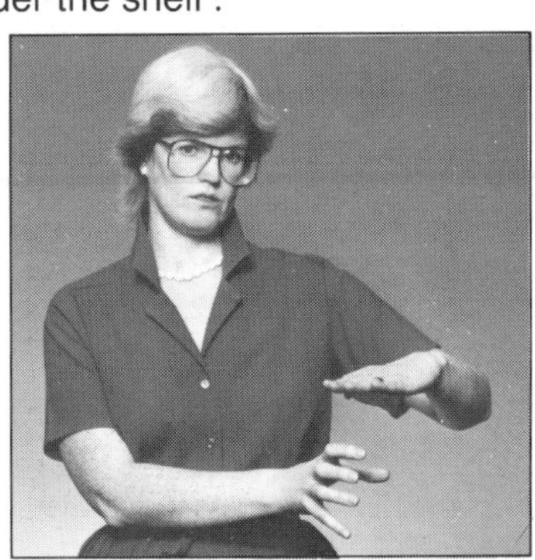

'ball under shelf'

In a more complicated description, the signer may place his signs separately, one after the other, but with the same awareness of where one image goes in relationship to another. The English sentence 'The house is on the hill' might be shown like this in BSL. First establish the hill, then add the house:

HILL

HOUSE

In these two examples, we see that the meaning of 'under' and 'on' are shown by where the different signs are placed. These signs may be modified to fit them into the image. Compare how the sign HOUSE is used here with the dictionary form given on p. 68. Here it is smaller, as well as being in a different place.

Let's add to the description:

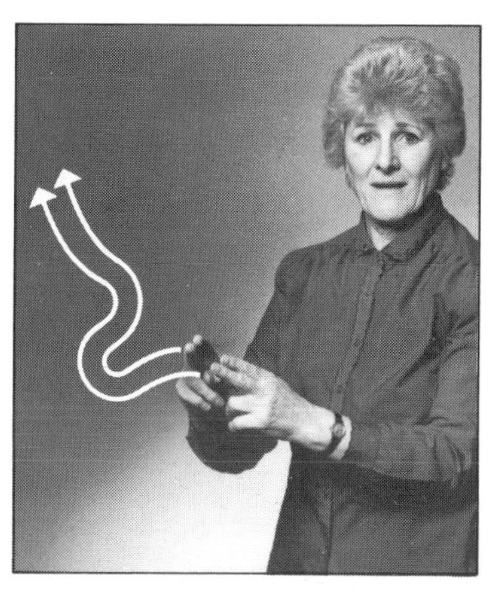

'A path up the hill'

'a road below the hill'

'a car parked on the road'

Again, the signs are placed and moved to show relationship in space. The sign PATH winds upwards in the area where the sign HILL was made, to give the meaning 'A winding path going uphill'. The sign ROAD is made on a lower level than HILL; and the proform for a parked car is placed where ROAD was made. Thus the information given can be translated into English as 'The house is on a hill, with a path winding up to it, and a road curves past below. Park opposite the path.' These signs might be placed in similar relationships in any part of the signing space to give this meaning.

Placement cannot be shown clearly without the use of pointing, eye gaze or body shift.

Pointing You have seen (p.77) that certain signs are made by pointing. For placement, once a signer has established things or people in the signing space, he uses these pointing signs to refer back to them. As long as he continues signing about the thing he has placed, he can refer to it again without giving its name, simply by pointing to the place in the signing space where he put it. This reference back is sometimes no more than a flick of the finger and can easily be overlooked.

Eye gaze and body shift These usually, but not always, go together. Both help to establish where different people, places and things are in relation to the signer. For instance, in reporting a conversation between two people, the signer will turn and gaze to the right for the first person's statement and shift to the left for the other person's reply. When she reports an exchange between an adult and child, that is what happens.

Simply by shifting the body to the left or right and the gaze up or down, she tells us whether it's the child or the adult who is signing. The same kind of role reversal allows the signer to portray the conflicting emotions of different people almost instantaneously. In the example below, the signer is first a learner driver, then shifts to become an impatient overtaking motorist who turns to glare at 'herself'.

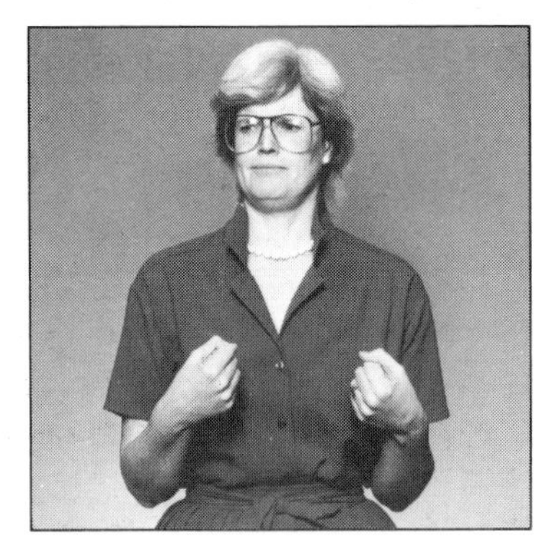

Eye gaze (which usually involves turning the head) can help to contribute precise meanings to a manual sign in context. The English sentences given with the examples shown below are possible translations of BSL sentences that depend on eye gaze for meaning.

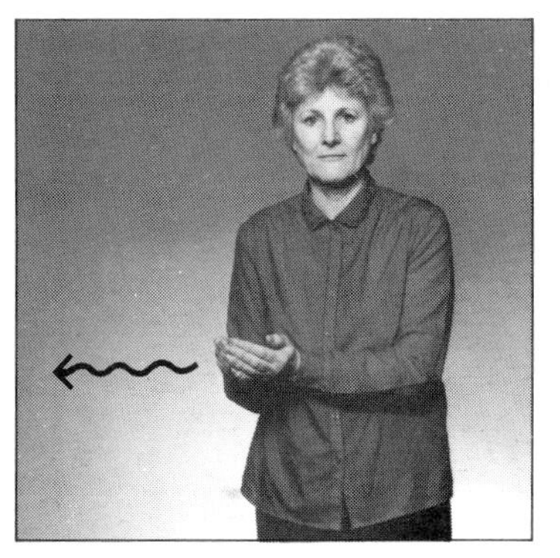

BOAT (basic sign)

'I was sailing to (. . .) by boat'

'The boat got away without being seen.'

From these examples, you will get some idea of the importance of eye gaze in adding to sign placement and in helping to link up meaning in BSL.

b) Sign direction

We have seen that classifiers and proforms can be moved easily in space, so that a person, crowd, or car can be shown to approach, move away from or go past the signers in various ways; lights can shine towards or away from, above or below the signer, legs can jump in any direction. This directionality, together with changes in the kind of movement, allows BSL to express a wide range of meanings.

If the hands, in position for the sign DRIVE (see p. 70), move forward smoothly, for example, the meaning of 'driving to . . .' or 'driving there' is given. When the direction of movement is sideways, the meaning becomes 'give (someone) a lift to . . .'.

This kind of directional movement can change what seems to be an object, or noun, into an action, or verb. When the hands, in position for the beginning of HOUSE, are moved towards the signer, the meaning becomes 'visit my house', and when moved away from the signer they imply 'visit your house, his house, etc.' according to the direction of movement.

'Visit my house'

Certain other BSL verb signs can be changed to show the difference between the subject and object of a sentence. In English this is done by word order: 'John looks at Marissa' means that 'John' is the subject who is looking at 'Marissa', the object. In BSL, if the signer himself is the subject (or 'I' in English) these verb signs will move or face away *from* him *towards* the object.

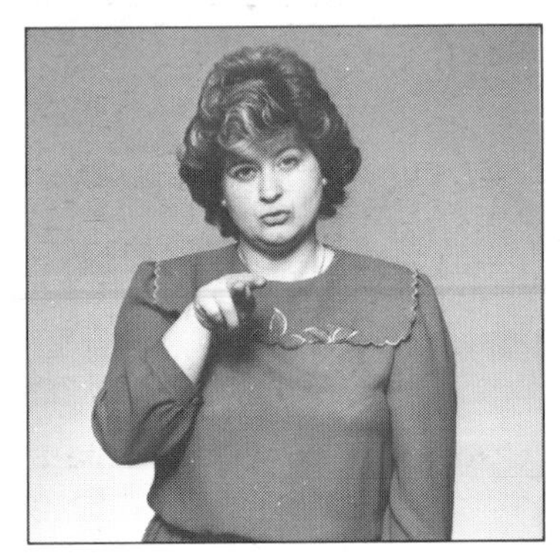

I-WATCH-YOU

I-ASK-HIM

If the signer is the object ('me' in English) the direction is reversed.

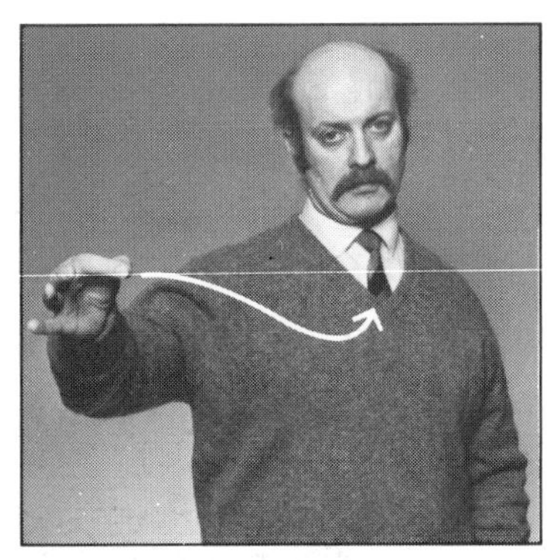

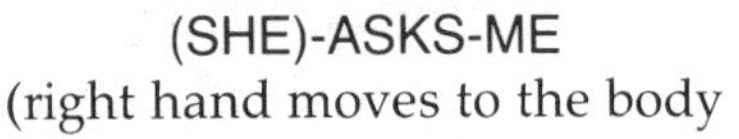

(SHE)-ASKS-ME
(right hand moves to the body

(HE)-WATCHES-ME

Among the verbs that change direction in this way are GIVE, TAKE, SEND, PAY, BLAME, NAG, TEASE, LEAVE-ALONE, and others. When the signer is neither the subject nor the object, the sign is still made from the direction of the subject towards the object, i.e.

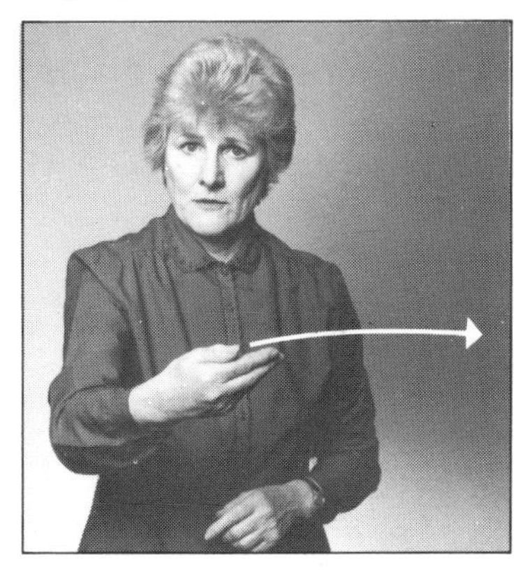

YOU-GIVE-(HIM)

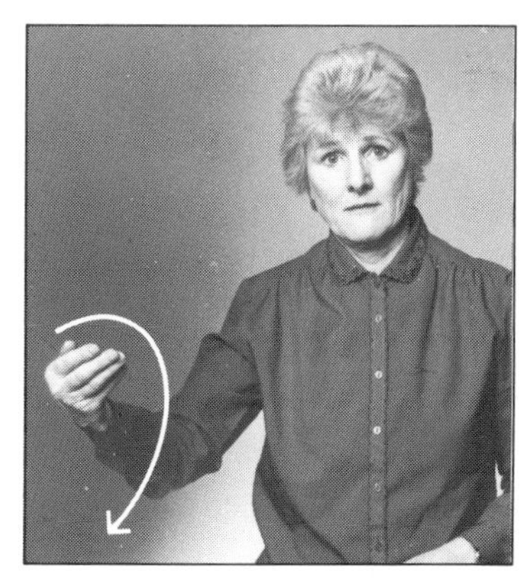

(SHE)-GIVES-YOU

How do we show more than one object? If I make the sign PAY towards you, it means 'I pay you'. But if I repeat it in several different directions it means 'I pay several people'. By omitting some directions I can show 'I paid certain people', and if I use a sweeping motion it means 'I paid them all'. Most of the verb signs listed above can be modulated in the same ways. This important use of sign direction to change meaning is discussed some more on p. 106.

'I pay you'

'I pay several people'

'I pay them all'

2 In sequence

In English, words have a definite order in a sentence. A speaker can only say one word at a time, so rules can be made about which word should come first. In BSL, as you have seen, two one-handed signs can be made at the same time, and further meanings can be added by other parts of the body simultaneously, as in this example, which in English is 'A huge wave covers the ship':

'huge'
(cheeks bulge)

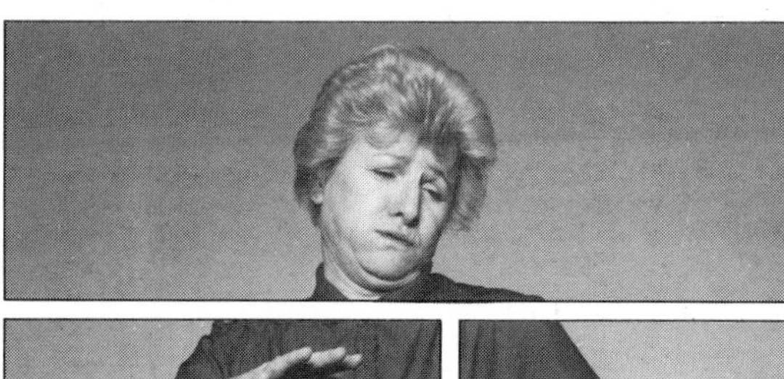

WAVE
(right hand)

SHIP
(left hand)

WAVE-COVERS-SHIP
(right and left hands)

This simultaneity makes it difficult to give rules about sign order in BSL, but there are some grammatical structures that can be described.

a) Pronouns

The signs ME, YOU, HE, etc. can be made at the beginning or end of a phrase or sentence. If made at the beginning, they are almost always repeated at the end, often seeming to be the final movement of the last sign in the phrase or sentence. This is rather similar to the way that Welsh people will say, for example, 'I've had enough, me'.

b) Clauses

To break up sentences into parts, signers sometimes use raised and knitted eyebrows, headtilts or nods. Such signals are also used for 'If . . .' or 'When . . .' clauses. Take, for example, the sentence: 'If she comes, I'll leave'.

In BSL, the first part of such a sentence ('If she comes . . .) would be signed with raised brows and head slightly tilted back, and the brows and head drop before the second part (. . . I'll leave').

c) Questions

These also require different eyebrow and head movement as you saw on p. 63. For WH- questions, the question signs, like pronouns, may be made at either or both ends of a question sentence, but fit most naturally at the end.

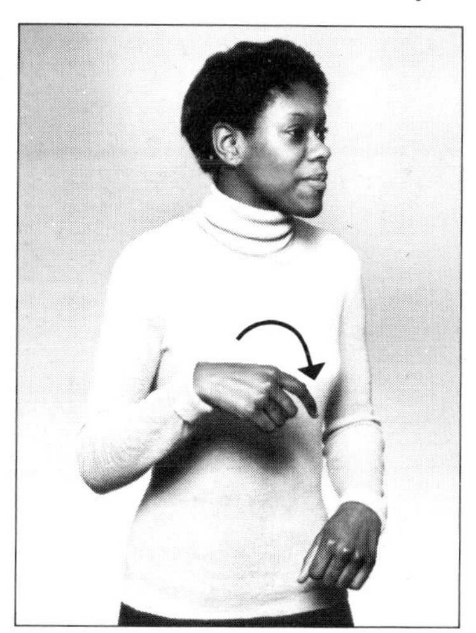

COME

WHAT-TIME

'What time are you coming?'

d) Topic-comment structure

Many BSL sentences have this type of structure. The signer gives his subject or topic first, then adds more information or comment. He may use raised eyebrows and a headtilt to identify his topic. If the topic of a discussion is someone's dress, that person might say in English, 'I bought this dress last year'. In BSL the signs would be arranged thus:

(brows raised, head tilted back)	(nod)
DRESS-THIS	(ME)-BUY-LAST-YEAR

The same English sentence, with different intonations, could be used if people were talking about last year's club jumble sale and what they bought. But then the BSL sentence would need to be arranged as follows:

(brows raised, head tilted back)	(nod)
(ME)-LAST-YEAR-ME	BUY-DRESS-THIS

As a beginner you should be safe using this topic–comment structure until you have picked up other ways of making sentences.

e) 'Film' sequences

To enhance the presentation in reporting and storytelling, BSL can use a different way of linking signs from the topic–comment structure described above. You saw in the section on placement of signs that a signer can build up a message through a sequence of visual images, not unlike the frames of a film. The order of BSL signs is sometimes very like the sequence of shots in a film, especially when reporting events, real or imaginary. Without having to think about it, a good signer produces the same effects as in film making, moving rapidly between close-up, mid-shot and long-shot. In 'close-up', the signer conveys meaning through his own face, head and body movements, supported by signs. He enlarges the area of focus to 'mid-shot', when he establishes other people or objects close around him, but still includes himself in the activity. In the 'long-shot', he injects additional movement and distance into his story by using more classifiers and proforms (pp. 72–74).

As he changes from one 'shot' to another, he may use the cut (a straightforward change of sign), the freeze (where one sign remains in the air while something else happens on the face or on the other hand), and even the zoom and fade. The result is a very vivid visual presentation. It must be said again, however, that the possible resemblance between a signed story and a film does not mean that BSL is a picture language. As a visual language it can come closer to another visual medium than spoken language can, but being able to tell vivid stories is, as you have seen, only part of what BSL can do.

f) Signs of the times

What about time? How is that handled in a visual language like BSL?

One of the most ingenious processes in BSL is its way of showing the many different aspects of time. In English, past, present and future are indicated by adding other words or endings to the verbs:

(past)	(present)	(future)
I walked	I walk	I will walk

BSL can also mark tenses in this way using the signs glossed as WILL, NOW and FINISH. Any statement that includes the sign WILL can be expected to refer to the future, NOW to the present and FINISH to the past.

But a far richer source of information about time is the use of different zones in the signing space to convey different ideas about the passage of time. These refer not just to past, present and future, but to clock and calendar time, hour-after-hour, week-after-week, year-after-year, and the passage of time in terms of human growth.

These zones are called *Time lines A, B, C* and *D*.

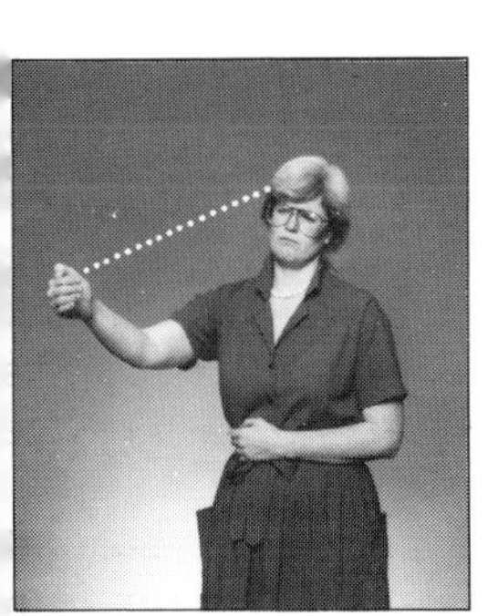

A (Past to future)

B (Short time units)

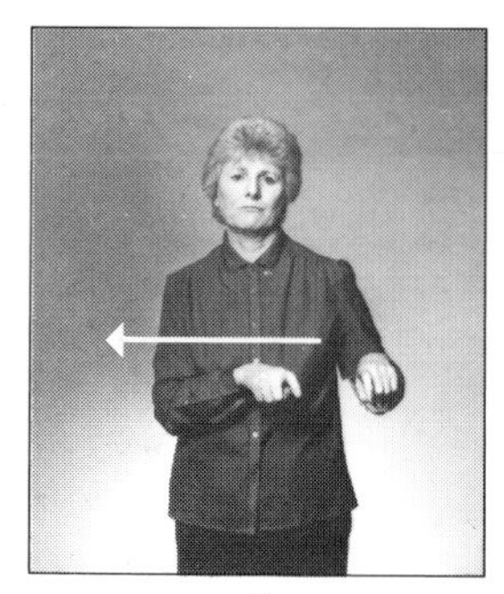

C (Continuing time)

D (Growing time)

Time line A runs from just behind the signer's shoulder to a foot or two in front of him. Signs made just above or behind the shoulder indicate past time. For the distant past, both hands circle *backwards* alternately, varying the number, size and speed of the circles according to the length of time being described. To show the passing of long periods of time, the hands circle *forwards*, but remain close above the shoulder unless present time has been reached. Signs meaning 'in the past' and 'recently' are made just above or slightly in front of the shoulder.

'in the past'

'long, long ago'

'time rolled by'

As might be expected, signs like YESTERDAY, TOMORROW, EVERYDAY, DAILY and the Scottish DAY are made on the face.

TOMORROW

EVERY-DAY

In the northeast area, signs related to 'week' also move outwards from the face. As time moves into the future, signs are made further forward, with a larger, slower movement usually indicating the distant future.

LATER

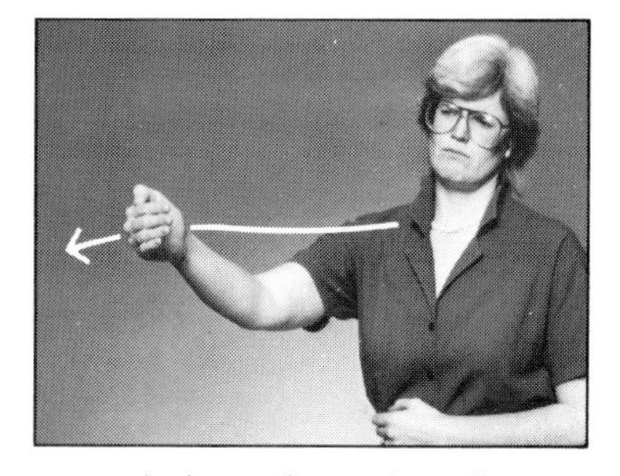

'a long time ahead'

Time line B runs along the left arm and hand in a right-handed signer. It is used to show some calendar time, succession and duration. For certain signs, the palm of the hand represents a clockface.

Calendar time includes weeks and years. The signs NEXT-WEEK and NEXT-YEAR, shown here, illustrate how the type and direction of movement gives specific meanings.

NEXT-WEEK

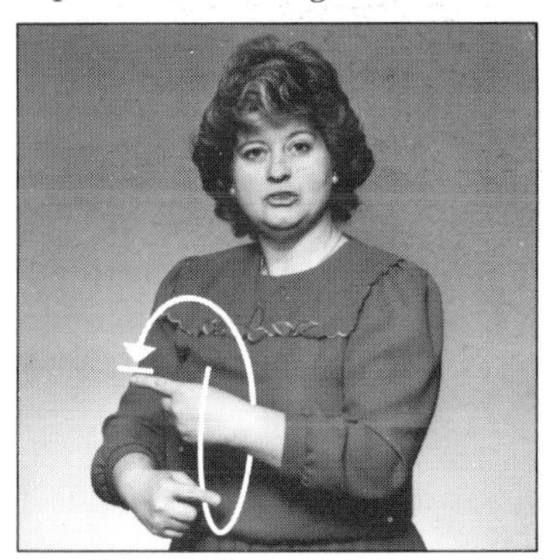

NEXT-YEAR

Other modulations give the following meanings:

Backward movement
= LAST-WEEK

Backward circle
= LAST-YEAR

Rapid backwards and forwards movement
= EVERY-WEEK

Quick continuous forward circle
= EVERY-YEAR

Forward movement returning as half-circle, slowly
= WEEK-AFTER-WEEK

Slow forward circle
= YEAR-AFTER-YEAR

The use of number handshapes with the above movements allows the signer to convey information such as:

IN-THREE-WEEKS

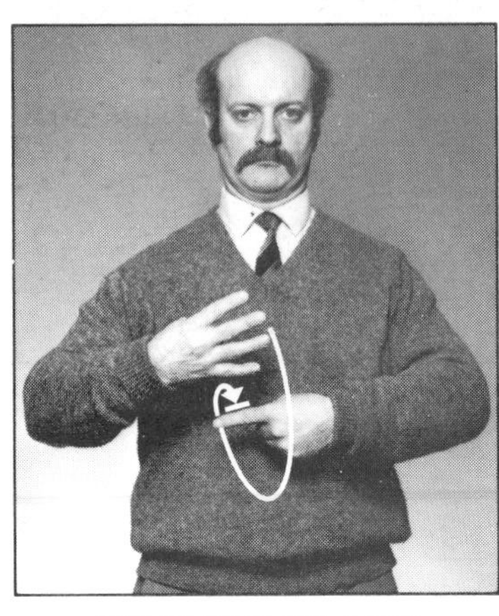
FOUR-YEARS-AGO

EVERY-TWO-WEEKS

For THIS-WEEK and THIS-YEAR there is a special modulation.

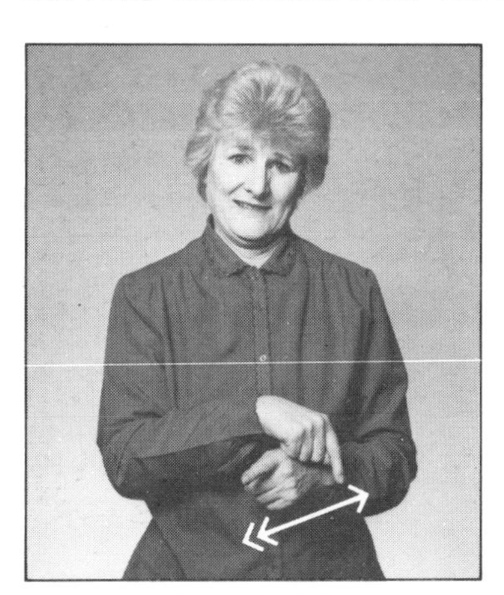
THIS-WEEK

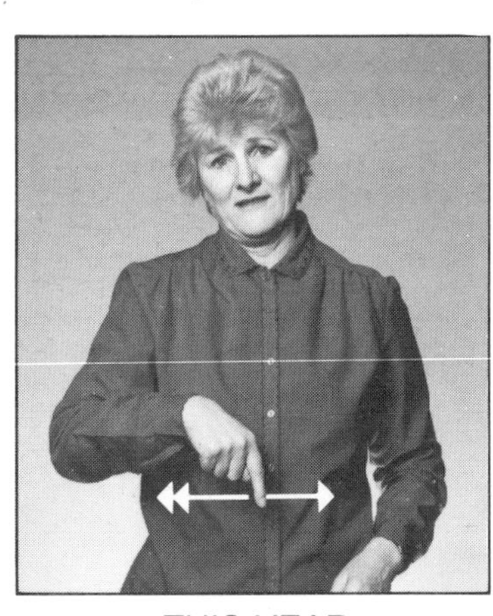
THIS-YEAR

For succession (BEFORE and AFTER) the right hand moves backwards or forwards from an imaginary line on the side of the left hand. Here are the two different handshapes that can be used to sign this:

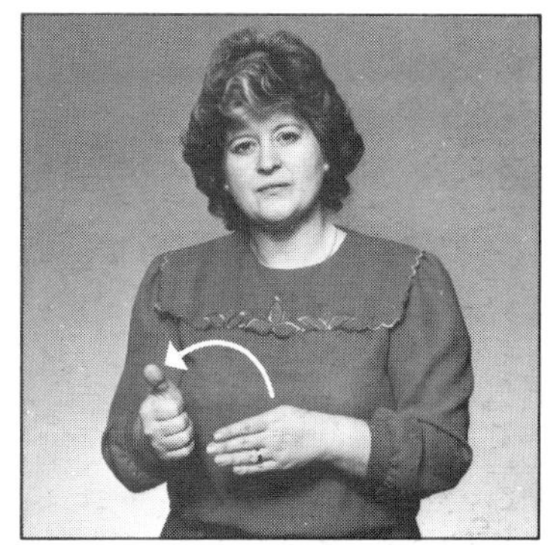

BEFORE (Handshape 1)

AFTER (Handshape 2)

(Left hand stays still)

A longer movement indicates concepts like 'a long time before (or after)', while short repeated movements indicate 'just before (or after)'.

Duration includes concepts such as 'a long time' (used in statements such as 'I've been waiting for a long time'); 'till' or 'until' (see illustration), and the passing of hours (described below).

LONG-TIME

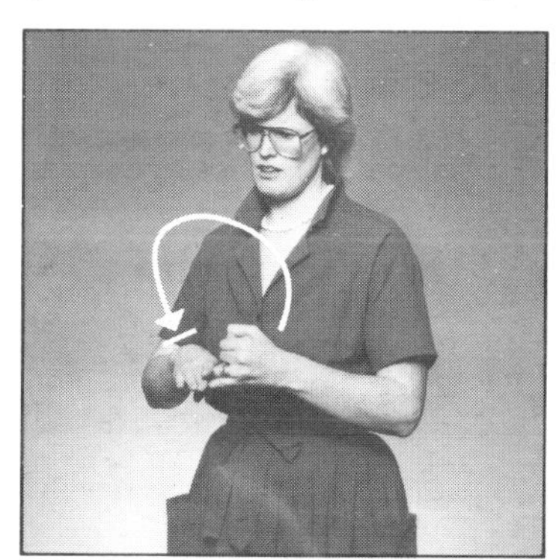

UNTIL

HOUR

The sign HOUR, shown above, has a brisk movement of the right hand around the left palm. When this movement is slowed down, it indicates that 'the hour dragged', and if speeded up, that 'the hour flew by'. A repeated circling shows HOUR-AFTER-HOUR, and if these circles stop at the top of the palm, this suggests 'once every hour', or a similar meaning.

Another possible way of showing the passing of clock time is to use the index finger to represent the clock's minute hand. This can then be moved to show minutes ticking by, or to give concepts such as 'after half an hour', and so on. When the tip of the index finger circles the palm several times rapidly (often with the whole sign moving to the right), the meaning 'for hours', or 'several hours passed' is indicated.

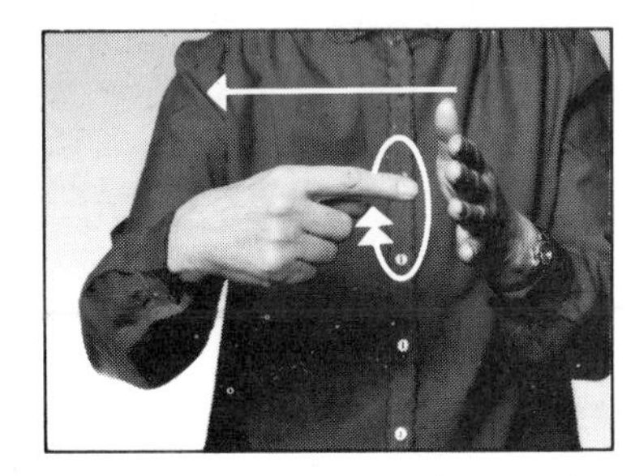

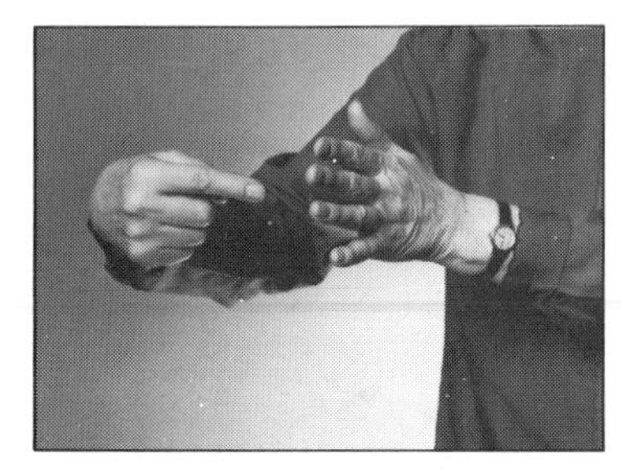

'several hours passed'
(The right hand makes repeated circles while the left hand follows it)

The 'minute hand' is also used in making the sign LATE, where the index finger drops suddenly down the palm. However, the opposite – EARLY – is not usually made by lifting the index finger, but belongs with concepts like 'quickly' and 'hurry'.

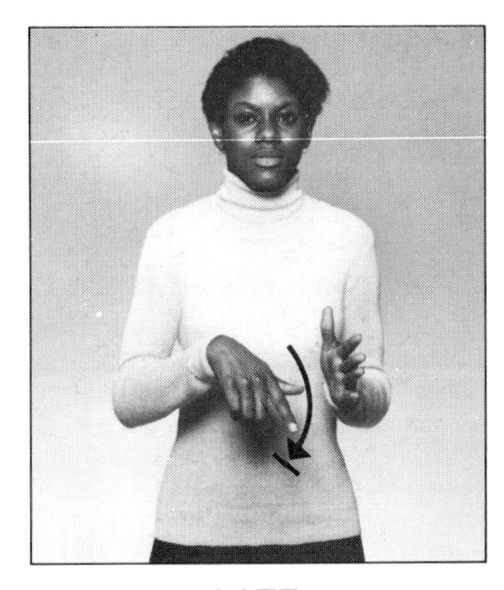

LATE

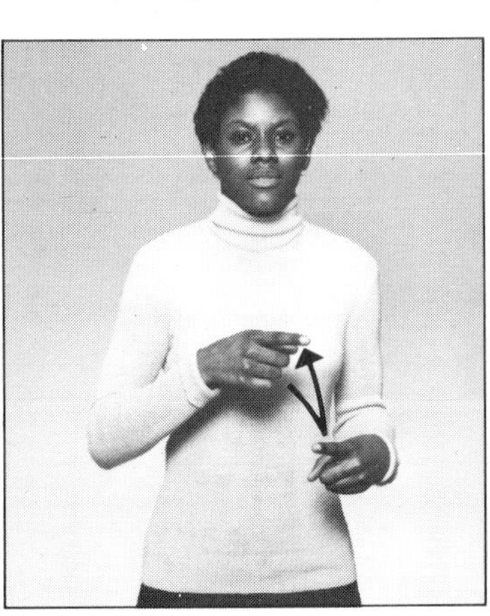

EARLY

In telling the time, number handshapes are used with special movements (see p. 81). For a time like 'twenty to four', the 'to' is usually fingerspelled, but sometimes signed as shown below, while in 'twenty minutes past four', these signs are used for 'minutes' and 'past'.

TO

PAST

MINUTE(S)

Time line C crosses in front of the signer. It is the place for the sign NOW/TODAY. Generally, however, it represents continuing time, particularly if the sign moves from left to right.

TODAY

CONTINUE and FOREVER are two of the signs that move along this line. Other signs using this line can be translated as 'repeatedly', 'not for a long time', 'remain fixed', 'delay' and 'for that period'.

CONTINUE

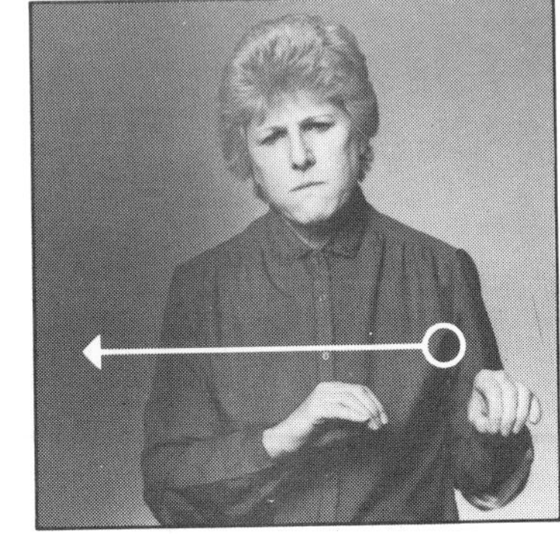

'not for a long time'

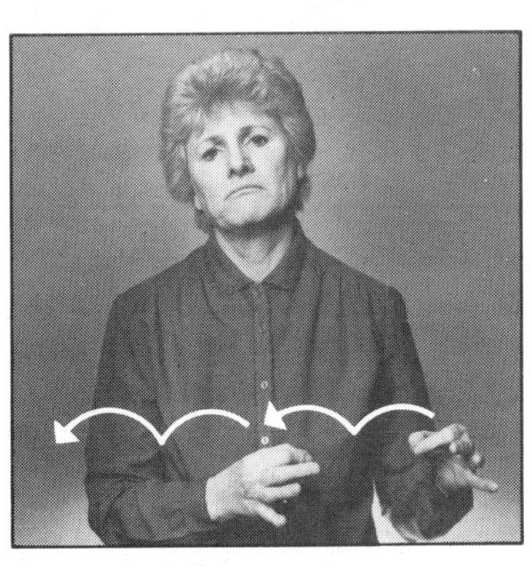

DELAY

'for that period'

Time line D The main use of time line D is to show something growing up or growing to maturity. Signs like SMALL, TALL, CHILD(REN) and ADULTS are made at certain points along this line, while for concepts like 'grew up' and 'all my life' the hand moves upwards. Passage of time can also be indicated by shorter movements. When two hands are used in 'grew up' the meaning becomes 'grew up together'. In descriptions like 'from the time I was 3½ till I was 7', the signer gives the beginning age, then makes an upward movement between the approximate heights for the two ages, and gives the final age to complete the information.

When a slow movement is used it can mean that the period of time dragged for the person referred to, or that something was happening continually and persistently in that person's life as he or she was growing up.

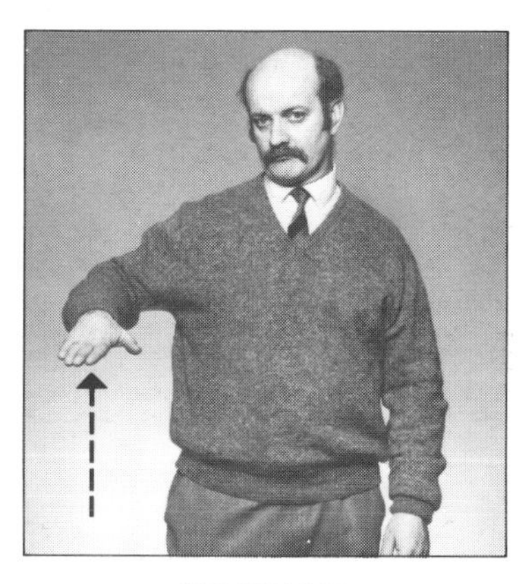

GROW-UP

Changing times BSL uses time itself to add meaning to some of its messages. It does this by sign repetition, and by different patterns of movement and speed.

Repetition is sometimes used for plurals, e.g. the sign GLASS can be repeated to make GLASSES.

GLASS

GLASSES
(left hand moves underneath right hand)

More often, repetition is used with verb signs to show that something happened more than once. You have seen (p. 93) that the sign PAY can be directed towards one person, several or many. If this sign is done repeatedly in any direction with a normal rhythm it means 'to pay regularly'. If the movement is rapid and short, it means 'to pay often'. A slow, circular repetition implies 'pay for a long time'. With these and other patterns, supported by facial and body information, BSL is able to give a whole range of precise messages about different kinds of time.

PAY-REGULARLY
(repeated forward movement)

PAY-OFTEN
(fast forward repetition)

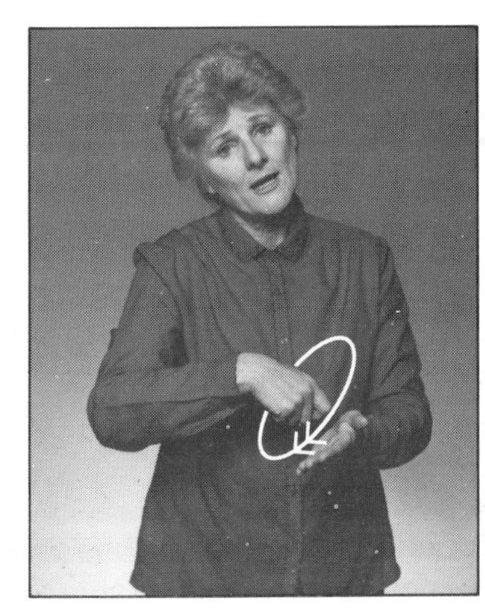

PAY-FOR-A-LONG-TIME
(slow forward repetition)

Signing Off

You are now aware of most of the main features of BSL. You know something about how it works, and what groups of signs you can expect to see frequently. The Programme Notes on p. 112 will give you more information about BSL and the deaf community and will also help you to follow the BBC Television series. Above all, don't be put off by so much information! Find a local teacher and mix with deaf people who will help you practise. As you learn the language, everything will gradually fall into place. Happy signing!

GLOSSARY OF TERMS

arbitrary: Describes a sign that is not iconic, i.e. has no visual resemblance to its meaning.

area vision: The ability to see what's going on in a large area, while looking directly at only one point.

articulator: A part of the body used to produce speech, or signs. For example, the hands are one articulator of signs.

body shift: In Sign Language, movements of the body, especially turning in different directions, used when describing the actions or reactions of two or more people. (See *role shift*.)

cochlear implant: A recently developed idea, whereby a totally deaf person has pieces of metal placed inside the head and body to bypass the deaf nerves of the ear. The operation allows some people to hear noise, which they can then use to interpret their environment. It does *not* enable people to understand speech. The danger of cochlear implants, which are still in the experimental stage, is that they will be increasingly carried out on children who are not able to make informed decisions about such an operation. The whole issue of cochlear implants is a controversial one and there are opposing views.

combined method: A late nineteenth-century term used to describe the combined use of signs with spoken language for teaching purposes, developed in response to oralism. (See *Signed English, Signs Supporting English, Total Communication.*)

configuration(s): Research term for the handshape(s) from which signs are made.

Creole: Creole languages are spoken in many parts of the world, but the best known in England is that used by West Indian communities, where two or more languages are in everyday contact and so a pidgin language is developed to bridge the gap between them. The children of the pidgin-users then develop it into a full language, known as a creole. A creole therefore has the potential to slide up and down a scale between two languages, being more like or less like either of them at different times. This leads to a lot of misunderstanding about the status of the language, and users of a Creole often have a very difficult time in the English classroom.

cued speech: A system of signals used to aid lipreading.

culture: A set of customs, behaviours, beliefs, needs, preferences, etc. developed within a group, which can be passed on from generation to generation.

deaf club: A centre where deaf people meet regularly.

deaf community: A group, which may be local, national or international, made up of people who use sign language and who identify themselves with other members.

Actual hearing loss is not the most important criteria for membership. Fluent signers, hearing or partially hearing, may be more accepted than non-signing deaf persons.

directional signs: In British Sign Language, those signs (especially verbs) that are moved in different directions to show relationships, e.g. of subject and object.

eye contact: Two people looking directly at each other. This is necessary for the beginning of a signed conversation, for interrupting, punctuation, and so on.

eye gaze: The direction in which the signer is looking. This can add information to the sign, and also help with *placement, role shift* and other features.

film sequences: The author's own term to describe one way of linking meaning in British Sign Language. In a story or description, visual images can be linked like the shots of a film, with close-ups (information given only by the face, head and body), mid-shots (objects and people 'established' around the signer), and long-shots (the use of classifiers, proforms and iconic signs).

fingerspelling: The use of certain handshapes (in Britain, made with two hands) to represent letters of the written alphabet; words made in this way. (See *manual alphabet*).

Gestuno: Sign vocabulary selected or adapted from various sign languages, for use during meetings and formal gatherings by officers (and members) of the World Federation of the Deaf. Dictionary published in 1975.

gesture(s): Movements of the hands and body that have developed differently in different cultures, are produced differently by different people, and are used mainly to accompany and emphasise the spoken word. Without speech, they cannot normally be linked together to give meaning.

gloss(es): English word(s), printed in this book in capital letters, which are used to label a sign, e.g. BOOK. The English word may have several meanings, and the gloss may refer to only one of them, or vice versa, so glosses should not be confused with words.

handshape: The shape of the hand when a sign is made. (See *configuration*.)

iconic (sign): A sign that is similar to the figure, shape or action of the real thing, e.g. SCISSORS (see pp. 67–72).

integration: Educational policy of placing 'disadvantaged' children into ordinary schools and classes. Considered to be of doubtful value in the deaf community because this does not guarantee that every child will pick up English, or even communicate well enough to make friends, and also because it means deaf children are isolated from each other and from knowledge of the deaf community. Integration often means that the weaker group is forced to accept the values of the dominant group without question which is not acceptable. Steve Biko, the campaigner for Black rights in South Africa, was referring to this when he said 'we don't want integration, we want de-segregation'.

linguist: A person who studies language or knows several languages well.

linguistic minority: A group of people using a common language and living in the same country, whose numbers are smaller than the rest of the population. Often these groups are dominated by the majority language; hence the need for United Nations rulings to protect them from being destroyed.

linguistics: The study of languages. By using the established tools and techniques for studying spoken languages, it was possible for linguists to show that sign languages worked just as well as spoken languages, though in a different way.

lip patterns: Movements of the lips that accompany certain signs. These may be borrowed from English words, or be special to British Sign Language (pp. 62 and 82). Also called *mouth patterns.*

lipreading: Understanding a spoken language by following the lip patterns of the speaker. Less than half the speech sounds of English are shown on the lips and lipreading is a skill that not everyone can master.

location: The place where the hand is put when a sign is made; also, within the signing space, the place where a person, object, etc. is 'set up'.

Makaton vocabulary: A language programme comprising a core vocabulary of essential concepts. Used extensively in the UK and overseas, with signs, symbols and speech, to facilitate communication and language in people with severe communication problems and learning difficulties.

manual: Of signs, that part of the sign that is made by the hands (p. 54). (See also *non-manual features.*)

manual alphabet: The 26 letters of the written English alphabet formed on the hands (see p. 83).

mime: Acting something out in a stylised way, without words or signs.

modulate, modulation: Altering a sign in some way to change its meaning.

mouthing: Making the mouth movements of English speech without sound.

mouth patterns: See *lip patterns.*

movement: In Sign Language research, this refers to the direction, type, speed, etc. of the movement *within* a sign.

multi-channel sign: A sign which gets its full meaning from more than one channel, e.g. from the hands and face at the same time. Also used to describe those signs which cannot easily be translated into English (previously called British Sign Language idioms), as these are all multi-channel signs. (See *non-manual features* and *simultaneity.*)

negative face: Standardised facial expressions used with many negative signs or statements.

negative incorporation: Changing the meaning of a sign from positive to negative, by using a negative face and/or headshake, or by changing the end movement of a sign, e.g. HUNGRY, NOT-HUNGRY (p. 64).

negative signs: Any sign that can be used to give a negative meaning, e.g. NOTHING (p. 79).

non-manual features: Information given when a sign is made by any part of the body other than the hands, e.g. face (mouth, cheeks, eyes, eyebrows), head, shoulders, upper body.

number incorporation: This refers to the use of number handshapes within other signs, e.g. EVERY-TWO-WEEKS, SEVEN-YEARS-OLD, etc. (p. 100).

oralism: A philosophy in the education of the deaf which maintains that language should be oral, i.e. from the mouth, and consequently that sign languages and deaf teachers should be excluded from the classroom. In its extreme form, oralism even discourages contact between deaf adults (club-joining, marriage, etc.) and criticises the public use of sign language.

orientation: Term used in research for the direction in which the palm and fingertips of the hand are facing when a sign is made.

Paget-Gorman Sign System: A sign system used in certain schools and classes for the deaf to provide visible English. It was created by a few individuals without reference to the deaf community and has no relation to British Sign Language.

Partially Hearing Unit (PHU): A unit in a hearing school offering assistance to partially hearing children.

peripheral vision: See *area vision*.

pictorial (sign): See *iconic*.

placement: In sign language, the setting-up of people, objects or places in space in relation to the signer or to each other, for reference or during descriptions of real or imagined events.

place of articulation: Term used in research for the place where the hand or hands are put when a sign is made. (See *location*.)

positive face: Standardised facial expression used with many positive signs or statements.

proforms: Handshapes that can be used to take the place of other signs, because they are more easily moved in the signing space.

receiver: See *watcher*.

referents: People, objects or places that have been 'set up' in the signing space and can be referred to by pointing.

regional variations: Differences in signs used in different parts of Britain to mean the same thing. Similar to dialects and accents in spoken languages.

role play: In sign language, this means taking different parts in a description or story.

role shift: Changing from one role to another in a description or story. (See *body shift*.)

sender: Person who is giving a message; a signer.

sign direction: See *directional signs*.

Signed English: A form of visible English which uses the sign vocabulary of British Sign Language, often with additions to show English word endings, tenses, etc., in English word order. (See also *Signs Supporting English*.)

signer: Person using sign language.

signing space: The area on or around the body within which signs are made.

sign language: A visual means of communication used within a deaf community and learned naturally by interaction, which is not dependent on a spoken language.

sign location: See *location*.

sign order: The order of, and relationships between signs to give meaning in a sign language. (See *film sequences, topic-comment, syntax*.)

sign system: Artificially created signs used to match the words of a spoken language; restricted number of signs, which do not change, developed for a special purpose, e.g. tic-tac signs at racecourses.

Signs Supporting English: Similar to signed English, but uses fingerspelling or lipreading rather than added signs to complete words in English word order.

simultaneity: In sign language, messages given by the hands, face, etc. contributing information at the same time.

syntax: The order of, and relationship between words (or signs) to give meaning in a language. (See *sign order*.)

time lines: The lines on which most time signs are made, including:

A – Distant past to future time;
B – Recent past to future;
C – Continuing time;
D – 'Growing' time.

(See illustration p. 97.)

topic-comment structure: A way of linking meaning in British Sign Language, where first the topic is given, often with a special eyebrow movement to mark it, then a comment follows.

Total Communication: A philosophy calling for every possible means of communication to be used with deaf children – technological aids (hearing aids, visual aids), English (speech, lipreading, fingerspelling) and signs (signed English, British Sign Language). In practice, Total Communication is often used to mean signed English – English blended with signs.

translucent sign: A sign that does not look very much like the thing it represents, but which can be recognised as such once its meaning is known.

transparent sign: A sign which gives a clear visual image of the thing it represents.

watcher: Person receiving a signed message.

WH-question: A question using words like 'what', 'who', 'where', 'why', and so on, requiring information from the other person.

Yes/No question: A question such as 'Are you hungry?', requiring the other person to say 'yes' or 'no'.

PROGRAMME NOTES

Introduction

These notes will help you to follow the BBC series on British Sign Language, and also to find further information about the language in the main chapters of this book.

Meet your presenters (and friends)

Lorna Allsop

Lorna Allsop comes from Bristol and is a native signer: that is, she acquired BSL in the way most children acquire their first language, by communication within the family and with those around her. Lorna is among the minority (approx. 10%) of deaf people whose parents and other relatives are also deaf, so she grew up with BSL.

Clive Mason, who is also deaf, is already known to national television as a presenter for *See Hear*, the popular BBC Sunday magazine show dealing with the events and concerns of hearing-impaired people in general and the deaf community in particular. He is a Scotsman born and bred, works in London but lives near Coventry.

Clive Mason

During the programmes you will be glimpsing other signers, among them *Rachael Bell* of Newcastle, now living in Didcot; *Wendy Daunt* of Birmingham; *Jerry Hanifin* from Manchester; and *John Lee*, who like Clive works for *See Hear*. Of these, Rachael and John are native signers, though John is not himself deaf. Growing up with deaf parents, mixing in the deaf community as well as in the hearing environment of school and neighbourhood, he became bilingual in BSL and English at an early age. Now he serves as an interpreter for *See Hear* and other programmes.

Clive, Wendy and Jerry represent the majority of BSL users, those who picked up the language from older children in schools or units for the deaf. Often, because communication in a hearing environment is limited for the profoundly deaf child, BSL is the true first language of such persons.

BBC Video

A video which includes the material in the series plus extra demonstrations and examples is available from:

BBC Video
P.O. Box 433
Portishead
Bristol BS20 9SG

For enquiries regarding the video, telephone:
01-576 0202 Ex 2236.

Programme One

Your presenters, Lorna and Clive, introduce you to some basic facts about British Sign Language using demonstrations.

First, any questions? Here are some that are often asked:

IS SIGN LANGUAGE INTERNATIONAL?
IS IT SPELLING OUT WORDS ON YOUR FINGERS?
IS IT A KIND OF MIME?
WHAT HAPPENS IF YOU ARE LEFT-HANDED?

You should be able to find the answers to these and similar questions, either in this book or from the programmes in the series. For example, the answer to the first question can be found on pp. 47–49; and Lorna answers the last question during this programme. If you are left-handed, just do what comes naturally and let your left hand lead (don't switch from one to the other).

Mime and BSL

Is BSL just mime? Sometimes there is a resemblance, but Jerry Hanifin demonstrates how different the two really are. Notice that in miming he uses real space and time, and real action. He goes through the motions of pressing the accelerator, of getting out of his car, walking around to where the front of the car would be, lifting the bonnet and propping it open, and so on. For BSL he stays in one place and uses a limited number of hand and body movements to convey the idea of space and action, taking far less time than in acting it out. So BSL is not the same as mime, although it uses the same visual channel.

Signed and spoken languages

How different is a visual language from a spoken one? You will be finding out as the series continues, but one way in which it is *not* different is in its potential to deliver a vast amount and variety of information. It is the way such information is given that is different. As Lorna points out, instead of *talking* about the weather, in BSL you can *see* it happening. Clive gives an example (see page 138 for a translation). You can read about other differences on pp. 50–54, but for this programme they can be summed up as follows:

Speech uses sound, which is received by the ears; speakers do not need to watch each other. BSL uses visual signals or messages, which are perceived by the eyes, so signers need eye contact.

Speakers stand close to be within earshot of each other; signers like more space to make and see the signs.

While speech is formed within the vocal cords and larynx and framed by the tongue and lips, signs are made within a specific signing space (see p. 53), and the hands use only certain movements and shapes to make signs within this space.

Look for other differences in later programmes, and enjoy exploring this vivid new language.

At the end of Programme One, you will know a little more about what BSL is or isn't; have had your first opportunity to see and attempt a signed phrase; and be ready to find out more . . .

Programme Two

Lorna, with Clive, shows you why the signs of BSL shouldn't be confused with everyday gestures used by speakers. They show how each sign has a specific handshape, but that certain handshapes can be used in several different ways to give different meanings. Your presenters also demonstrate that using BSL is not like drawing pictures in the air.

Gesture and sign

In spoken languages, the only obvious movement is of the lips; in BSL, messages may be sent by movements of the hands, arms, face, head and body. Fleeting changes of facial expression can add important information.

The gestures used by English speakers when talking to each other don't mean very much on their own. They are often invented on the spur of the moment by the person who is talking, and are forgotten as soon as they have been made.

The signs of BSL are not like that. Each is made with a specific handshape in a specific place moved in a specific way. (More than 50 handshapes have been listed, but only about half of these are used to make most of the signs.) So signs, unlike gestures, are not invented on the spot or quickly forgotten (see pp. 54–58). Your presenters concentrate in this programme on a few of the handshapes to show what can be done with them.

Sign 'families'

Clive helps Lorna to demonstrate how certain handshapes, which on their own have a basic meaning, can be used to provide a family of related meanings. So the thumbs-up handshape (*above right*), which is associated with the idea of 'good', can be placed in different locations and moved in different ways to give us meanings such as 'agree', 'know', 'sweet' and many others. But the same handshape can also be used for meanings that don't necessarily relate to good. Did you spot the odd-one-out in the demonstration? It was the sign translated as 'milk', which got its handshape in a different way.

The opposite of 'good' is suggested to signers by

'good' handshape

'you're wrong'
(hand moves towards person who is wrong)

the raised little finger (*below right*), which gives us 'I'm wrong', 'you're wrong', 'that's awful', 'I object' and so on in addition to 'bad'. (See pages 77–78.)

Next, Lorna and Clive show you a number of signs made with a flat handshape that has no separate meaning of its own in these signs. The signs they demonstrate that use this handshape include meanings such as 'to want', 'to like', 'please', 'thank you', and 'I don't know'. While you are learning BSL, you will automatically learn what handshape to use for each sign, along with its position and movement and which way it should face. Don't get too concerned about the separate parts!

Images in the air

Newcomers to BSL are likely to be excited by the fact that certain signs seem to give pictures (or images) of the ideas they represent. Often people assume that all signs are like this (*iconic*). If they were, they could easily be understood and learned, but Lorna and Clive demonstrate that this is not true. There are many signs that cannot be recognised unless you know their meaning (see pp. 66–67). As with any new language, there is no short cut to learning BSL – though you may have more fun while learning it!

Conversation time

Clive and Lorna give you more to talk about in this new language as they take refreshment. Here's the English translation of their conversation, but try to follow it without checking here as you watch. The words in italics underneath the translations show the actual sign order of BSL to give you an idea of how English and BSL sentence structure differ. Bear in mind that the words are only representations of the signs.

LORNA
Hello.

CLIVE
Hello.

LORNA
Would you like tea?
Like tea you

CLIVE
Yes please.
Yes (head nod) *please*

LORNA
Do you want milk?
(Point at milk) *milk want you*

CLIVE
No, thank you.
No (head shake) *thank you*

LORNA
Do you want sugar?
You sugar (head nod) *you*

CLIVE
Yes please.
Good yes (head nod) *please*

LORNA
How many?
How many you

CLIVE
Three.
Me three

LORNA
Three! That's terrible.
Three. Terrible you

CLIVE
I agree, but I like it sweet.
I agree, but me taste sweet like me

By now you will know more about how individual signs are made. You should also have increased your sign power sufficiently to accept an invitation to tea with a signing acquaintance!

Programme Three

In this programme your presenters look at differences between the way information is given in English and in BSL. Remember that BSL is a visual language, so expect things that you are not familiar with for spoken language.

Topic-comment

All languages use different kinds of sentence structure, but usually one type is seen as most common. In English this is the SVO sentence (subject-verb-object), as in the sentence:

Julia caught a fish
(subject) (verb) (object)

Another type of sentence is called topic-comment. This is used in English when someone points out a person or thing (the topic) with a lift in the voice, then goes on to give information about it (comment). For example:

That fish – Julia caught it
(topic) (comment)

The topic-comment sentence is not the most common type used in English. But in BSL it is used so often that BSL has been described as a topic-comment language. By giving the topic first, the signer is then able to focus attention on the comment that follows.

In the programme we see Clive signing a topic-comment sentence, which is given here in direct English translation to show you the order. (Remember that BSL normally has no spoken or written form so the English words given here only *represent* signs.)

CAR THAT-ONE RED (IS) MINE

HOUSE THERE BIG MY FATHER BEEN BUILT

The topic is usually accompanied by raised eyebrows and a lifted chin, then the eyebrows/chin drop for the comment. See if you can tell where the topic ends and the comment begins. (See also pp. 95–96.)

Instant information

In English, words must be spoken one after the other, i.e. *in sequence*. BSL, like other sign languages, uses two hands, the face and facial features, the head, the body and space itself to give information. In this way, it can provide several pieces of information at the same time or *simultaneously*. Rachael Bell demonstrates one example of this simultaneity for you, in which she gives information about a ship in a stormy sea. She can tell us not only that a wave covers the ship, but also in what direction the ship and the wave are moving, how high the wave is and so on. (See also p. 94.)

No match for each other

The above examples of topic-comment sentences and simultaneity help to show that BSL works in a different way from English. It is often possible to match individual signs with single English words, such as 'red' or 'where', but when these signs are used in context they may have other meanings, and many complex ideas are expressed by only one sign. The idea given in English by 'Someone came up to me' is presented in BSL by the raised index finger moving through space towards the signer, not by single signs for each English word.

So we can see that English words and BSL signs cannot be matched on a one-to-one basis. And though it is possible to speak English and use some signs at the same time (see p. 37), when this match is attempted, the result is not BSL, nor is it often good English.

Conversation time

Lorna introduces some basic conversational sentences for beginners, and Clive and John help to demonstrate them and give you practice. Lorna reminds you that you may see some signs not used in your area. Here is the English version of Clive's final conversation with John. See how much you can follow without relying on this translation.

JOHN
Hello.

CLIVE
Hello. Are you deaf?

JOHN
No, I'm hearing.

CLIVE
Where are you from?

JOHN
Near Birmingham. Where are you from (yourself)?

CLIVE
I grew up in Glasgow.

By the end of this programme, you will have begun to see some of the differences between how a spoken language like English and a visual/ gestural language like BSL present information. You will also have seen your first short conversation in BSL and will perhaps be looking forward to trying it out with a deaf person. And you may get a compliment –

CLIVE
You sign well. Where did you learn?

Programme Four

In Programme Four, Lorna and Clive introduce signs related to the family. And they demonstrate how fingerspelling is used in British Sign Language, for family signs among others. Lorna talks about name signs, and Clive tells you a story.

Happy families

In any small community, the ties of family and friendship will be important. Although the BSL community is scattered around the country, its members come together often at the local, regional or national levels. Intermarriage among signing deaf people is very common, and the children of such marriages (whether deaf or hearing) may join their parents in community activities at an early age. So the sense of family within the BSL community is strong, and the signs referring to family relationships are, if not standard, at least very similar throughout Great Britain.

A family might be made up of a man, a woman, a boy and a girl. Clive demonstrates signs that are used for these individuals, and for people in general. And he shows that certain other signs, such as those representing a child, adolescent or adult, are made by indicating the approximate height they may have reached.

Then Lorna and Clive introduce the BSL family, beginning with the sign for 'wedding'. Lorna explains that the signs meaning 'mother' and 'father' are among those that are made by borrowing the initial letter of the English word: 'm' for 'mother', 'f' for 'father' and so on. How is this done? Through fingerspelling . . .

Words in hand

BSL has a means of showing each letter of the English alphabet visually, and they can then be used to spell out the names of people and places as necessary. This is done through a two-handed fingerspelling system (sometimes known as the manual alphabet) which has a hand arrangement to represent each letter. Signers don't spell out each letter of a word separately, which would be like someone saying 'Bee-eye-el-el' instead of Bill. As they form one letter they are already preparing to make the next one, so that the letters run together in patterns to create words. The reader of fingerspelling looks for these patterns, not the letters.

You will best learn to make and recognise fingerspelling patterns at a class where a deaf teacher can give you practice with short words such as names. Learning in other ways may result in establishing habits that can't be broken. Fingerspelling cards that show the 26 hand-arrangements in alphabetical order (see p. 83) are useful if you need to check what you've already learned, but cannot show you how to weave one letter into another. So if you want to spell well (and sign well) join a class.

Your fingerspelling skills will come in useful if you are discussing days of the week or months of the year. The signs for these (in most regions) are based on the initial letter or first few letters of the English word. You will learn which other signs make use of fingerspelling as you go along. Remember, though, don't think of fingerspelling English sentences as a substitute for BSL. There are two different languages involved here.

Show me your name

Fingerspelling can be used to spell out anyone's name in English. But many signers have a BSL name too. This is a name sign created (perhaps by family members or school friends) to capture some characteristic of its owner. For example, Lorna's almond eyes explain her sign, and Jerry's derives from the fact that his name looks like 'cherry' on the lips. Name signs are usually personal to the individual – after all, how many Lornas will have almond eyes? – but some common name signs do occur (see p. 85).

If you join a local class you may be given a temporary name sign to be used on the course, just like the ones given to the class shown in the programme. You won't have to accept a name-sign that you don't like, so you shouldn't worry if it turns out to be permanent!

Story time

To complete the programme, Clive tells the following story in BSL.

There was a family – father, mother and son. They lived in Glasgow, and Father was out working, Monday to Friday. But with work over for the week, he was happy and quite excited. The family piled into their large, expensive red car and drove off at speed, Father at the wheel. They were going well until Father took a wrong turning and got completely lost – he didn't know where they were. So he turned to Mother sitting beside him and said, 'I'm totally lost!' 'Hold on a minute!' said Mum, and opened up the map. She showed it to their son who was sitting in the back seat and asked him if he knew where to go. He showed her on the map which way to go, and she turned back and relayed the directions to Father.

'Where?', he demanded anxiously, but at last he got back onto the right road and drove at full speed till they arrived in London. And the reason for this journey to London was to go to their daughter's wedding. All the members of this family were deaf, except for the daughter, who was hearing.

You have learned a number of signs that can be used in discussing families. And you have seen other signs that are made with fingerspelled letters. Have you wondered what name sign you might be given in a class?

Programme Five

This programme concentrates on numbers from one to twelve. It should be a simple matter – but for the fact that in BSL the number signs vary from region to region. Lorna and Clive explain a little about regional dialect before they demonstrate some of the special uses of numbers.

Dialects

English speakers accept the fact that different words and phrases are used in different parts of Britain to mean the same thing. Dialects like Geordie, Yorkshire, Somerset and Glaswegian may take a bit of getting used to for the outsider, but they are accepted as variations of English. The same is true with the regional dialects of BSL. Most signs are used or recognised by the majority of British signers, but about one-fifth are found only within specific regions (or are in the process of change). This variation in no way limits communication, since signers adjust to each other quickly, just as most speakers do.

One, two, three . . .

The several different number systems in BSL are familiar to many signers, especially those who attend national gatherings. Some can switch from one to another with ease. So whatever number system you may learn in your local area, you should be able to use it elsewhere as long as you are aware of possible differences.

During this programme, the number system you will see is used in various parts of the country including the Midlands, London and the south (see pp. 79–81). The important thing to watch for is how these numbers can provide other information in various ways:

When the sign starts at the chin and moves forward, the number refers to pounds (money).

To show age, the number sign moves away from the nose or cheek.

For time, the sign has a twist to it (and sometimes a special movement – see p. 81).

Note also the handshape that looks like the number five, with wiggling fingers. This, depending on five, with wiggling fingers. This, depending on where it is placed, can be used to ask 'how many', 'how old', 'when' and other number-related questions (see p. 82).

Conversation time

Here's a translation of the conversation:

CLIVE
How many children are coming?

LORNA
Twelve.

CLIVE
How old are they?

LORNA
Most of them are six (years old).

CLIVE
How many adults?

LORNA
There's myself and two more. Three altogether.

CLIVE
Do you want any help?

LORNA
Yes please. How many hats are there?

CLIVE
Twelve.

LORNA
How many balloons?

CLIVE
Ten.

LORNA
I need two more.

CLIVE
Were these things cheap?

LORNA
No, they were quite expensive. The hats cost £3 and the balloons were £2.

CLIVE
What time's the party?

LORNA
Two o'clock. What's the time now?

CLIVE
Half past twelve.

So now you have an idea of how numbers are used in BSL. Clive tells us a story about two people who meet by chance after some years. Look out for number signs. A translation is given on p. 138.

By now you should be aware of regional variations in BSL and be prepared to learn your local dialect, including the number signs. You can ask and answer questions about any amount, age and time when you learn further numbers.

Programme Six

After a brief introduction to international sign languages, Lorna and Clive devote this entire programme to demonstrating one of the main features of BSL: 'placement'.

Is sign language international?

This common question about sign language receives an answer. You get a glimpse of representatives from many different countries attending the most recent Congress of the World Federation of the Deaf held at Helsinki, Finland. The signers may seem at first glance all to be using the same language, because their channel of communication is the same (visual/gestural), and they have many rules – or features of grammar – in common. But though these similarities allow them to adjust to each other's communication much more easily than speakers can, each sign language is clearly separate. (If you watch the different interpreters at a congress like this, the fact becomes very obvious.)

Putting things in their place

One of the rules, or features, that many sign languages share is *placement*. This means the way signers use space to describe where things and people are in relation to each other.

How does English manage it? Professor Harlan Lane, an American psychologist and author, gives examples to show that the spoken word doesn't always offer a clear idea of the relative position of people and things.

Sign language is much more efficient at it. Lorna, with Clive, demonstrates how a signer establishes the position of items in space from a particular point of view, then is able to refer back to each item according to where it was in the signing space. The items may be things on a table or shelves, a landscape with buildings as described by Wendy (for translation see p. 138), people in the street, or almost anything (see pp. 88–91). Because signers use space itself, they are able to show visually how close or far away items are from each other, how far above or below, on which side, where they move to, and so on. Lorna tells us it's important to remember that when someone is explaining an arrangement of objects, or describing a scene, that the signer is giving the description from his point of view. Clive tells us about meeting a man and woman in the street:

It was quite a small street. I was walking along on one side, and there were two people walking towards me, one on each side of the street. The one on my side was a man, and the other was a woman. The woman crossed over, and they both came up to me. This one (the woman) was wearing glasses.

Then Clive describes a scene from a recent production of *A Christmas Carol*. Scrooge is sitting asleep in his room on Christmas Eve.

Scrooge is sitting down in a chair asleep, wearing a night-cap which is hanging down the right-hand side of his head. To his right there's a table with a candle and a book on it; there's also a decanter of wine and a glass on the table. Opposite him there's another seat, and to the left of that there's a table with a candle. There's a fireplace on Scrooge's left with a clock in the centre of the mantlepiece and a row of books beside it on the right. There's also a picture on the wall above the mantlepiece, and two candles on the wall. To the right of the fireplace there are some curtains, and behind Scrooge there is another set of curtains.

You should be able to spot other examples of placement as the series goes on because it appears so often in BSL.

In this programme you will have focused on, and learned more about the idea of placement. Perhaps you can try to describe some items in your own surroundings using the sign vocabulary learned in this and previous programmes.

Programme Seven

With spoken language, most people use nods, headshakes and different kinds of facial expression as part of their everyday communication. In BSL, such head movements and expressions often become part of the language itself. Lorna and Clive demonstrate with some examples.

Yes, no, positive and negative

As an English speaker, you will often shake your head while saying 'No' or nod while saying 'Yes'. Sometimes a nod or shake alone will give your meaning; this is certainly true in BSL. But signers also use these head movements to make positive and negative statements. If the sign translated as 'thirsty' is accompanied by a vigorous nod, it becomes 'I *am* thirsty', while a headshake with the same sign gives the meaning 'I'm not thirsty'. So a headshake can have an independent meaning similar to 'not' or 'don't'; and a nod sometimes means more than just 'yes' (see p. 64). (See p. 138 for translations of the examples.)

Question time

Many speakers also use specific facial expressions, especially when asking questions. These expressions may be quite unconscious and are less important, in English, than a rising intonation in the voice. In BSL, the expressions can take the place of vocal intonation, and are essential for questions (*above right*).

For a question that expects an answer of 'yes' or 'no', your brows are usually raised and your eyes may widen a little.* Test yourself with these questions in English and in their BSL translations:

Do you drive?
Are you hungry?
Are you hearing?

For WH-questions (the kind that, in English, start with WHAT, WHERE, WHEN, WHY, WHICH, WHO or HOW), the eyebrows usually lower to a kind of frown and the eyes narrow to match (*right*).

* Note: If a yes/no question is asked with concern (e.g. 'Are you hurt?'), the eyebrows are more likely to be lowered than raised.

'Are you deaf?'

WHERE

This expression may vary according to how much you want to know the answer, but it encourages the other person to provide information in reply. Here are some examples that are given in BSL on the programmes:

How will she get here?

Where's the knife?

What's the time?

Remember that in BSL, the sign representing the WH-question usually comes at the end of a sentence (see p. 95).

Lorna and Clive have two different conversations involving questions. See how much you can understand without the voice-over.

CLIVE
(*finishes a conversation on a visual telephone*) Oh, hello. That was your mother. She wants to come over to your house for dinner.

LORNA
When's she coming?

CLIVE
Tomorrow evening.

LORNA
What time will she get here?

CLIVE
About seven (o'clock).

LORNA
How will she get here? By car?

CLIVE
By train.

LORNA
Train? Why?

CLIVE
Her car's broken down.

LORNA
Oh. I see.

(Clive and Lorna are sitting at a table. Clive is reading. Lorna taps the table to attract his attention.)

LORNA
Where's the knife.

CLIVE
Behind the teapot.

LORNA
Give it to me please. Thank you. Which mug is yours?

CLIVE
The red one.

LORNA
That one?

CLIVE
Yes.
(Lorna is about to pour tea *and Clive waves to attract attention*)

CLIVE
What's the time?

LORNA
Nine (o'clock).

CLIVE
I'm late! I must go!

Lorna explains that raised eyebrows and an upward tilt of the head can convey the same idea as the English word 'if'. Watch for the way Clive uses his face, head and shoulders in these examples:
'If he comes here, then I'll leave';
'If it's raining tomorrow, it'll be impossible to work'.

Now look out for questions in Rachael and Wendy's conversation about enrolling to teach BSL (see p. 139 for a translation).

In this programme, you saw how 'Yes' and 'No' could take on more meaning, and how expressions may serve as a kind of 'visual intonation' when questions are asked. Through conversations, you saw questions being asked and answered.

Programme Eight

In Programme Seven we saw how facial expression is used with questions. Now you'll see how facial expression changes the meaning of a sign.

How do you feel?

To show the degree of your feeling about something in spoken language, you may change the tone of your voice as you say a word such as 'like', 'angry', 'interested' and so on. Of course, you may also add other words such as 'so (much)', 'very (much)', 'extremely' etc, which emphasise your feeling. In BSL, a signer can show the degree of his feeling by facial expression, usually accompanied by changes in head and body movement or in the speed of the sign as well. Clive shows how much he likes different food dips by his expression.

What is it like?

Lorna explains that facial expressions can also tell signers how heavy or big something is, whether there are few or many objects or people, and so on. We see Clive describing how he lifted a light object and a heavy object, and the information about the weight can be obtained from the face alone. With his cheeks puffed out, Clive can indicate a great amount of food on his plate, a crowd of people, or a very tall building. A huge fish doesn't need to be described with outstretched arms if the face shows how big it is. Sucked-in cheeks and/or a pursed mouth indicate small or thin objects. (See also p. 61.)

How is it done?

Clive showed us a facial expression that means something like 'unconcerned' or 'casual'. He uses it with the sign translated as 'to walk'; but the same expression would give the same meaning if he were describing work, driving, reading, painting and so on. You can compare it with the expression used to show speed, that requires concentration. Clive then demonstrates the difference between looking at something suspiciously, looking intently, or with boredom. These expressions, and many more, can be used with other actions to give the same meanings (see pp. 59–60).

One-to-one conversation!

When you have tried out some of the expressions shown by Lorna and Clive for yourself watch Clive's stories. The first is about two drivers: one careful and patient; the other frustrated and angry.

I was in my car driving along calmly, and I looked in the rear-view mirror, and another car came screaming up very close behind me, and the driver was flashing his lights furiously. It was frightening. He kept moving around behind me trying to get past, so I moved over to the left. He pulled out and passed me, and gave me an absolutely furious look as he sped off. It was terrible.

The second story is a conversation between a husband and wife. Note how he acts out the two people, shifting his head and gaze from side to side as he becomes each character (see p. 90). This is another device in BSL, doing away with the need for 'So he said to me . . . and I said to him. . .'.

There was a (married) man who was very excited one morning in the kitchen as he prepared breakfast. When that was done he wrote out a card. He really had set everything out specially. Then his wife came downstairs, opened the kitchen door and looked in amazement at what was going on.
'What are you doing?' she asked.
Her husband looked surprised and said, 'Well, today is our wedding anniversary.'
'What!' said his wife.
'Yes, it's definitely today'
His wife said, 'No. Your're wrong.'
The husband was really disappointed and upset. He turned away and began to feel rather angry. He told his wife that he was upset she'd forgotten, then turned away again, angry. His wife then laughed mischievously to herself, picked something up and tapped him on the shoulder. He looked round and said, 'You did remember. You've been teasing me.' He was then really pleased and gave his wife a big hug.

You have now learned more about the information to be gained in BSL from the face (and head and body too). As Lorna says 'with a bit of practice you'll discover that using facial expression in BSL becomes second nature'.

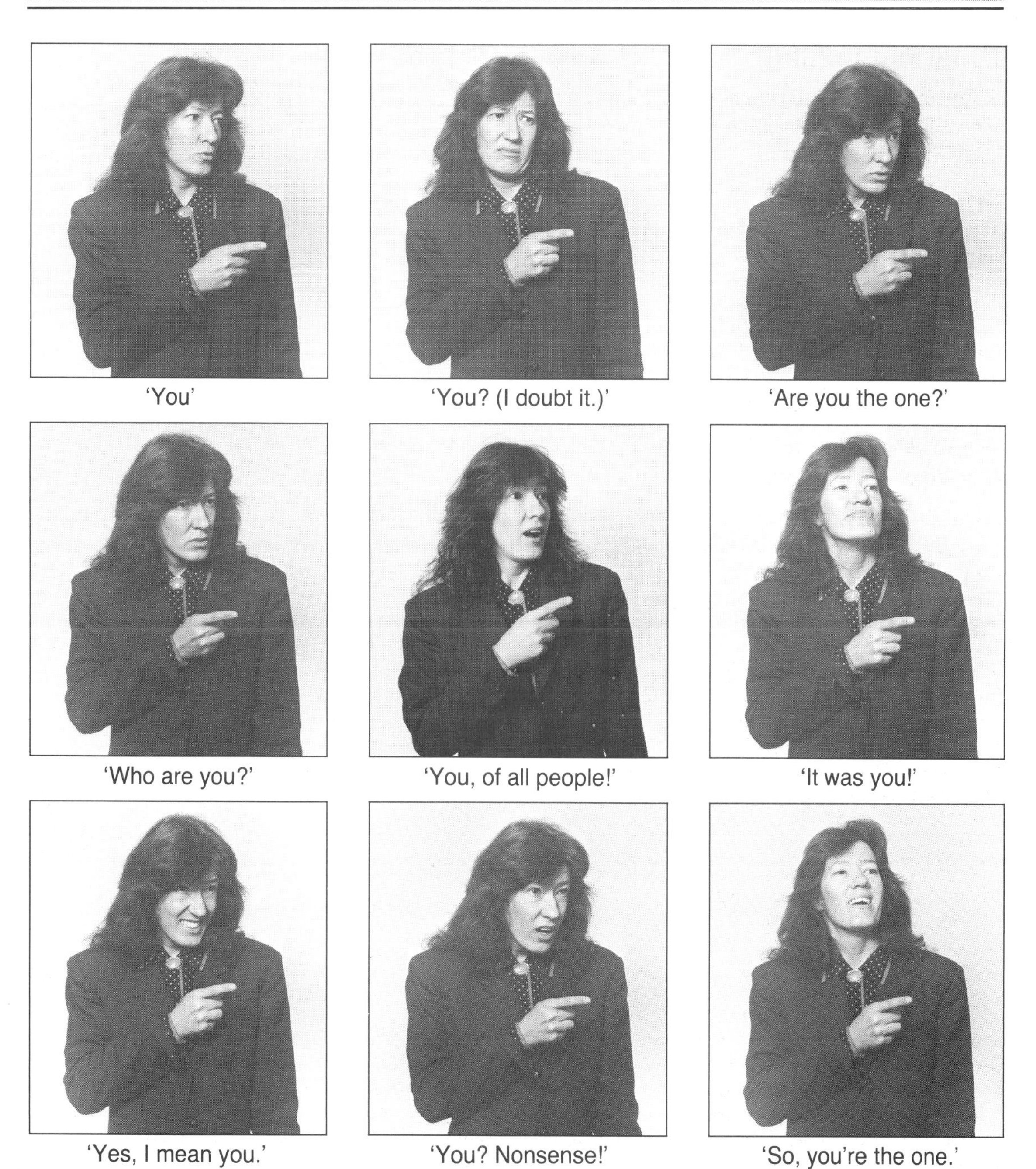

'You' 'You? (I doubt it.)' 'Are you the one?'

'Who are you?' 'You, of all people!' 'It was you!'

'Yes, I mean you.' 'You? Nonsense!' 'So, you're the one.'

These nine photographs show how different expressions can give the same (manual) sign different meanings.

Programme Nine

You have already seen how BSL deals with clock time. In this programme we look at other ways of talking about time, in relation to past, present and future. Lorna and Clive demonstrate several examples of signs made along imaginary time lines.

Then, now and later . . .

In English, you can usually show past, present and future by making changes in your verb. For example, you can say that something happen*ed* (then), is happen*ing* (now) or will happ*en* (later). Likewise the verb 'to work' can become 'I worked', 'I am working' and 'I shall work'.

In BSL (and several other languages, both spoken and signed), time is arranged differently. A sign that relates to an action such as work cannot be changed to show *when* the work was done. We saw in an earlier programme (Programme Eight) that, with a certain facial expression, a sign can show us *how* an action is done. Sometimes the movement of the sign itself does this; so Clive can demonstrate the difference between hard and easy work. But he can't make similar changes to show whether he works hard in the past, present or future.

Instead, he must give information to help establish his position in time before he describes an action. To talk about work, he may begin by using signs that 'set' the time, such as those that mean the same as:

> a long time ago, now, next year;

or

> yesterday, today, next Friday

and so on. If he starts with 'next year' we know that his work and anything else he talks about will be happening in the future. When he wants to change to the past or present, he must first give us new information about time. Under this arrangement, it is not necessary for the sign relating to work to show *when* it happens, only *how* it happens.

WORK

A-LONG-TIME-AGO

BSL is a visual language, so it makes use of space to give information about time. Four imaginary time lines are arranged in the space around the body, each covering a different type of time period (see pp. 97–105). Lorna and Clive show you some of the signs made along three of the time lines, and you have a chance to fit past, present and future into your own signing space.

Conversation time (about time!)

Read this, not *before* or *during* but *after* you have watched Lorna and Clive talk about their activities.

LORNA
Hello!

CLIVE
Hello! I haven't seen you for a long time. What have you been doing?

LORNA
I've been very busy recently. Last week I was travelling all over the place; yesterday I was out filming; and today I had a meeting that went on for hours and hours and hours. I'm exhausted!

CLIVE
What about tomorrow!

LORNA
Tomorrow I've got to write a report.

CLIVE
What about next week?

LORNA
Next week's different. I'm off on holiday.

CLIVE
That's great!

To round off, Jerry Hanifin recounts the history of manned flight from the distant past to the present, and speculates about the future. A translation is given on p. 139.

You should now be able to use the vocabulary learned in previous lessons to talk about things that happened in the past, are happening now, or will happen later. One more programme to go! Have you found a class yet?

Programme Ten

The focus in this final programme is on 'direction' in BSL. As Lorna and Clive demonstrate, this means more than just giving directions from one place to another. It can also provide precise information about different actions, and change the meaning of certain signs in various ways.

Where do I go?

To you, the most familiar use of direction in BSL will be that of giving and following directions. Signers can often provide very detailed and accurate directions, because their visual language can reproduce the journey they are describing. Clive and Lorna demonstrate this through role play. If you join a sign class you may learn how to give the same sort of precise visual directions, or at least be able to follow them.

LORNA
Hello.

CLIVE
Oh! Hello.

LORNA
Where's the telephone?

CLIVE
Oh, OK. Right. Down this corridor there are some double doors on the left. Walk to them and push open the left-hand door. On the left are some stairs. Walk up there. Turn right and you come to double doors. Pull the door open, walk through and turn left. You come to a single door. Pull that open and there are several doors on the right. Not the first, not the second, but the third is the one. Walk to the door, push it open and there's the phone.

LORNA
Thank you. Bye.

Which way am I going?

Another part played by direction is to show which way people or objects move in space. (You will remember Rachael's ship (Programme Two) sailing one way, and the wave moving another way.) And

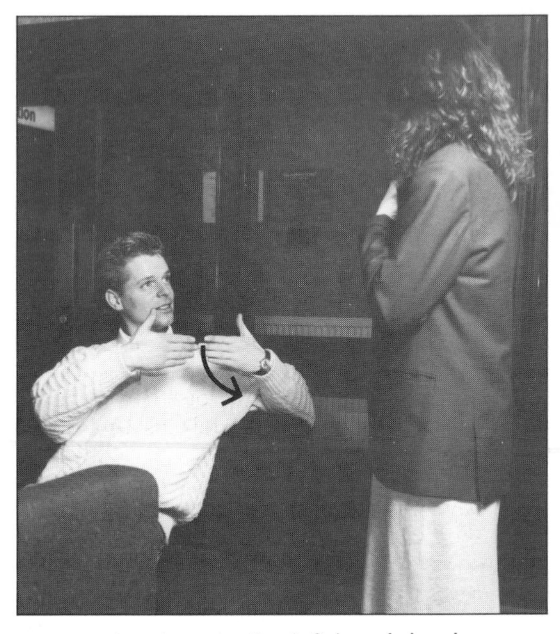

'push open the left-hand door'

Clive shows that by changing the direction of movement he can talk about a person going upstairs away from him, coming downstairs towards him (or any other possible arrangements for that matter).

This relationship between the sign and how things actually move in space is basic to BSL. Learners don't always grasp it right away, but with practice it should become more obvious.

Who am I talking about?

We saw in Programme Six that a signer can place things or people in space just as he can move them about. When the signer wants to refer back to a person or object already established in the space around him, he can simply point to or glance at the appropriate position in the signing space. Or his signs themselves may move in that direction, as you see in the next item. In these ways, direction can tell you who the signer is talking about very specifically.

Changing direction

The meaning of a sign can be changed in various ways by its direction. Jerry shows you several signs made with a fist handshape (which has the basic meaning of holding or possessing something). When Jerry moves this hand towards himself he gives the same meaning as the English 'my' or 'mine'. Moving it in other directions gives the idea of 'your', 'hers', 'theirs' and so on.

Another kind of changing direction is shown through the question sign related to 'which'. This sign can be moved back and forth between the objects to be chosen, in any direction (side to side, up and down, circular and so on). This kind of directional movement is very handy, as it gives a lot of information at once.

The same is true of certain signs that act in the same way as verbs like 'ask' or 'give' in English. When the signer is doing the asking or giving, the sign moves from her or him in the direction of the other person or persons. To show that he or she is being asked or given something, the sign moves from the direction of the other person towards the signer. In the same way, the direction of the sign can show 'he gives her', 'she gives you' and other combinations. BSL has many of these directional signs, which are easy to use once you get the idea (see pp. 92–93).

Off we go!

Lorna prepares to set off on the London Underground with Clive telling you what's happening. See how many examples of direction you can spot!

We come to the end of the series. But let's hope that your interest in BSL is just at the beginning. You can find out about your nearest BSL class by writing to the address below. As Lorna says, attending a class is the best way to get started and it's fun. So as we sign off – sign on!

BSL Classes

If you want to join a BSL class, write, enclosing a large s.a.e., to:

Into Sign
P.O. Box 12
Carlisle
CA1 1HU

You will then be sent a list of classes in your area.

BOOKLIST

BAKER, C. and BATTISON, R. eds *Sign language and the deaf community: essays in honour of William C. Stokoe* Silver Spring, Md: National Association of the Deaf, 1980.
BRENNAN, M. *et al. Words in hand; a structural analysis of signs of British Sign Language* Edinburgh: Moray House Publications, 1981. op.
FURTH, J. G. *Thinking without language* Collier-Macmillan, 1966.
HOUGH, J. *Louder than words* Cambridge: Great Ouse Press, 1983.
KYLE, J. G. and WOLL, B. *Sign Language: the study of deaf people and their language* Cambridge U.P., 1985.
LANE, H. *When the mind hears: a history of the deaf* New York: Random House, 1984
LYSONS, K. *The development of local voluntary societies for adult deaf persons in England* British Deaf News (supplement 1979).
PEPYS, S. *The diary of Samuel Pepys* (Vol. VII, 9th November 1666) Bell, 1972.
RUBINO, F. *et al. Gestuno: international sign language of the deaf* Carlisle: British Deaf Association; nd.
SAVAGE, R. D. *et al. Psychology and communication in deaf children* Sydney, Australia: Grune and Stratton, 1981.
STOKOE, W. C. *Sign language structure: the first linguistic analysis of American Sign Language* Silver Springs, Md: Linstock Press, rev. edn. 1978.
WOLL, B. *et al.* eds *Perspectives on British Sign Language* London: Croom Helm, 1981.

A full bibliography can be obtained by sending an s.a.e. to the address on p. 129.

Picture Credits

BRITISH DEAF ASSOCIATION Arthur Dimmock, page 38; BRITISH LIBRARY signs, page 16, title page, page 21, memorial, page 22; ROBERT BROEDER Charles I, page 66 (left); MARY EVANS PICTURE LIBRARY L'Epée, page 20, Sicard, page 21; ELISABETH FRINK 'Horse & Rider', page 66 (centre); GALLAUDET UNIVERSITY ARCHIVES Clerc, page 21; MANSELL COLLECTION signs, page 18, Bell, page 24; LAURENCE & LORNA MARSHALL Bushman signs, page 8; HENRY MOORE FOUNDATION 'Seated Figure', page 66 (right); NUD page 40; PATRIMONIO NACIONAL, MADRID de Navarrete's 'Adoration of the Shepherds' (detail), page 12; RNID cartoon, page 32; ROYAL INSTITUTION OF CORNWALL Carew, page 14; STIRLINGS OF KEIR COLLECTION de Navarrete, page 11.

SUBJECT INDEX

SIGN INDEX

See also 'outlines' and 'proforms' in Subject Index.
**Indicates signs not illustrated*

Translations of extra examples of BSL given in the BBC Television series

Programme One

I opened the curtains, looked out and, oh dear!, it was pouring with rain. So I closed the curtains – it wasn't very nice. Later, I opened the curtains and looked out again and, surprise! it was snowing gently.

Programme Five

CLIVE
One day, I was walking to my car in a car park. I was about to open the door, when I saw a red car parked next to mine. A man walked up to the car and I thought, 'I know him', so I waved to him and when he looked at me, I said, 'Are you deaf?'. And he said, 'Yes, I'm deaf.'
'Do you remember me?' I asked.
'Oh, yes, I remember you'.
So I went round the car and we shook hands.
We hadn't seen each other for ages, so I asked, 'When was the last time I saw you?'
He said, 'Oh, probably about twelve years ago.'
'That's right,' I said, 'Are you married now?'
'Yes,' he said, 'I'm married.'
'Any children?'
'Yes, I've got two children.'
'Tell me about them. How old are they?'
'Well, I've got a boy who's ten, and a girl who's seven.'
'Oh, tremendous! Are they deaf or hearing?'
'The boy is hearing and the girl is deaf.'
'Oh, right,' I said, 'What are you doing here?'
'Oh, I've moved here. I live about two miles down the road.'
'Really? When did you move?'
'Oh, about six weeks ago.'
'Great!'

Programme Six

Putting things in their place

WENDY
Last year I went to the school to look around, but I was disappointed to see all the changes. Before, the school building was here, with fields all around it, and over here the sports area for cricket, netball and so forth. Well, now houses are being built, popping up all over the place, and the grounds are getting smaller and smaller.

Programme Seven

Yes, no, positive and negative

Example 1

CLIVE
Do you have a car?

LORNA
Yes. Do you?

CLIVE
No, I don't

Example 2

LORNA (*waves to get attention*)
There's a lot of food, but I'm not hungry. Are you hungry?

CLIVE
I'm not hungry.

LORNA
Are you thirsty?

CLIVE
I'm not thirsty.

Rachael and Wendy's conversation

RACHAEL
May I have a piece of paper and a pen?

WENDY
Are you deaf?

RACHAEL
Yes.

WENDY
I'm deaf.

RACHAEL
Oh, I thought you were hearing.

WENDY
Don't stand, do sit down.

RACHAEL
About this (*points to notice*). I want to teach Sign Language here. I'm Rachael.

WENDY
Oh, yes – Rachael. I'm Wendy.

RACHAEL
Do those two over there teach Sign Language?

WENDY
Oh no. You and I.

Programme Nine

Long, long ago, when men wore beards, they would walk along and watch birds in flight. They'd watch the little birds flying round in flocks and see big birds flying through the sky, flapping their wings and then riding on the air currents. They'd watch a bird land and see how it landed, slowing down by pushing its wings forwards against the air. And, of course, man began to think about the possibility of flying himself. Eventually someone invented wings, which he strapped onto his arms, flapped to try them out and thought 'Yes, these might work!'. So, having put on the wings, he ran and flapped them and ran and flapped them, launched himself into the air and, of course, all he did was fall down to the ground again, failing to fly.

A long time after that, someone else had another idea and built a bicycle with a framework attached to it and wings. He put some goggles on, and then pedalled the bicycle as hard as he could, and the thing teetered from side to side as he went along, and eventually tipped over, collapsed, and the wings broke. So, once again, man had failed to fly.

A long time after that, someone thought of an aeroplane with two wings, a bi-plane with a propellor you had to spin by hand to get the engine going. The pilot sat in the cockpit with his goggles and said 'Right! Ready!'. The plane began to move along the ground and went faster and faster and the wings flexed and then it got off the ground, bounced back, got off the ground again and eventually managed to fly. So, at last, man had achieved flight.

Well, today, we have these huge, huge aeroplanes, like Concorde, and hundreds of people go in these things. Some even have two entrances, because there are so many to get on board. There are rows and rows of seats in the aeroplanes and they even show films during the flight. These planes taxi out onto the runway, and then with a huge surge of speed they race along the runway faster and faster and faster until they take off and then fly up into the sky, and then disappear into the distance.

In the future what's going to happen? Well, I, or you, might be boarding a rocket with lots of other people. And the rocket engines will fire, the rocket will go up faster and faster and faster and eventually fly to the moon. And then having landed on the moon, we can get out, wearing helmets and breathing apparatus and walk in the low gravity of the moon. And way, way down there we'll be able to see the earth and wave hello to it. That may well be what the future holds.

Translations of additional examples of BSL given in the BBC Enterprises video

Programme Three

Two different ways of describing the same situation are given. This is the translation for both versions.

I was sitting facing the Chairman. The Treasurer was sitting on my right, and the secretary was on my left.

Clive and John's conversation

CLIVE
What?

JOHN
Pass the milk, please. Thank you.

CLIVE
Are you deaf?

JOHN
No. I'm hearing.

CLIVE
You sign really well

JOHN
Well, I grew up with Sign Language. Both my parents are deaf.

CLIVE
Really? Where do they come from?

JOHN
From St Helens. Do you know them?

CLIVE
What's their name?

JOHN
Lee.

CLIVE
I don't know them. What's your name?

JOHN
My name's John. My wife's name is Carol. What's your name?

CLIVE
I'm Clive.

JOHN
Ah, Clive. Where are you from?

CLIVE
I grew up in Glasgow, but I live in London. Do you have children?

JOHN
Yes, two boys.

CLIVE
How old are they?

JOHN
Well, Ben is 7 and Timmy is 5. Are you married?

CLIVE
Oh, not yet.

Programme Four

Fingerspelled words demonstrated by Clive:

Bob; Max; joy; job; Pam; ham; law; tax; Tim; Tom; Ken; Sue; Vic; son; Fred; Gail; John; club; quiz

Programme Six

Clive tells a story about a mother and two children. Look for the way he uses placement.

A mother was at the sink washing up when she heard the loud noise of crying, so she turned to see what was going on.
'He's hitting me!' said the first child.
'I never did. He's a liar!' said the other one.
'Both of you stop it,' said Mother, hiding her amusement.

Programme Seven

LORNA
Now, let's look at a few more questions that might come in handy.

CLIVE
What do you want to eat?
What's wrong?
What's your job?
Are you married?
Did you go?
Have you got any money?
Where did you go on holiday?
Where do you live?

End Section

LORNA
To end with, we'd like to show you some useful phrases in BSL.

CLIVE
I'm sorry.
I apologise.
I forgot.
Can I interrupt?
I don't mind.
Sign that again, please.
I understand that bit, but what was the bit before?
You're signing too quickly. Please slow down.
Where do you live?
Do you remember?
I'm worried.
See you again.

As Lorna said, 'Remember, the best way to learn is to go to a class and be taught by a deaf tutor.'